Reshaping
the Media

Reshaping the Media

Mass Communication in an Information Age

Everette E. Dennis

SAGE PUBLICATIONS
The Publishers of Professional Social Science
Newbury Park   London   New Delhi

For information address:

SAGE Publications, Inc.
2111 West Hillcrest Drive
Newbury Park, California 91320

SAGE Publications Ltd.
28 Banner Street
London ECIY 8QE
England

SAGE Publications India Pvt. Ltd.
M-32 Market
Greater Kailash I
New Delhi 110 048 India

Printed in the United States of America

Library of Congress Cataloging-in-Publication Data

Dennis, Everette E.
    Reshaping the media: mass communication in an information age /
Everette E. Dennis.
        p.   cm.
    Bibliography: p.
    Includes index.
    ISBN 9-8039-3660-5. — ISBN 0-8039-3661-3 (pbk.)
    1. Mass media—United States. I. Title
P92.U5D45 1989   89-10509
302.23'0973—dc20   CIP

FIRST PRINTING, 1989

Contents

Preface

Anyone who administers an institute for advanced study is eventually asked to be a sense-maker, to provide a holistic picture that integrates fragments of singular instance into a coherent whole. As the head of the Gannett Center for Media Studies at Columbia University, I am frequently asked to explain what our inquiries into the media, their operations and audiences add up to. I do so in books, articles, speeches, and lectures as well as media interviews in an effort to keep track of the great issues, the central forces that bind media and people together. These efforts at sense-making have ranged from 20-40 second sound bites on network television to much longer presentations where I try to provide context and background for breaking stories about the media and public life.

Since 1984, requests for comment, in both short and long form, have taken me to other continents, scores of great universities and professional meetings and other forums. I have spoken at the Smithsonian Institution, presidential libraries, national conferences, press clubs, and civic groups. It has always been my goal to connect two kinds of knowledge — that gained by acquaintance with the media industries and that which has emerged from the work of media scholars — with media issues and problems of consequence to the public. Sometimes I get to choose my own topic; other times, I respond to requests from my hosts. I am guided by a conversation I had long ago with Dr. Karl Menninger, the eminent psychiatrist, who explained that he spoke only on topics he felt comfortable with, where he had enough knowledge to make sensible connections.

I have the good fortune to work in an environment where I am continuously learning. The Gannett Center attracts as fellows scholars and professionals who are among the world's experts in their respective fields. It is an international crossroads for visitors from scores of countries who come to get and impart information. And most importantly, we have an energetic and enthusiastic staff guiding and nurturing any and all work that emerges from our various programs.

Although I have spoken and written for many audiences from those communicated by satellite internationally to those that reached only a few people, most of these presentations have not reached the vast majority of people who are interested in communication media and issues. Author and press critic Alfred Balk has warned that media think tanks and study programs can become monastic cells unless they make a great effort to communicate their work to others. At the Gannett Center we do that daily in responding to calls from the media, through a lively publication program, mailings, correspondence; and by occasionally inviting the cable service C-SPAN to our conferences, meetings, and seminars. Still there is much good material that reaches a limited audience.

With that in mind, I have prepared this book based mostly on speeches, lectures, and columns, but substantially reworked and edited. There has been much help from Craig Fisher-LaMay, the Gannett Center's editorial manager, whose knowledge of communication and skill as an editor I value greatly.

My thanks go also to Eugene Dorsey, president of the Gannett Foundation; Gerald M. Sass, my immediate boss and the Foundation's vice president for education. I have benefited greatly from conversations with the 53 persons who have held fellowships at the Gannett Center, with many faculty members and administrative colleagues at Columbia University and from contact with scores of people in the news media as well as ordinary citizens who have come to my lectures and speeches. To all these people and others I am grateful. All but one of the essays are my own and appeared originally under my byline. The one exception is an essay in Chapter 2, "Walter Lippman and the American Century Revisited," which was co-authored with William A. Henry III of *Time* and Huntington Williams III of the *Gannett Center Journal*. At the Gannett Center, my former and current executive assistants, Mikki Morrissette Neff and Jackie Fleischer, deserve much credit for helping me navigate these essays betwixt and between other obligations and work.

—Everette E. Dennis
New York City

1

Sea Changes for the Media

A Coming of Age

The call which came from a woman who had been interviewed by the CBS News program *West 57th* was one of scores I have received in recent years from people eager to respond to or converse with the news media. This caller, a surrogate mother who felt she had been misrepresented, wondered how she could most effectively give her side to a story that had caused her emotional distress along with embarrassment among her friends and neighbors, not to mention millions of citizens elsewhere who heretofore had not been aware of her.

This and other conversations reinforce what studies of public attitudes toward the news media reveal: that public knowledge about the news media is modest indeed and that people are increasingly frustrated by their inability to interact with an institution they believe casts a large shadow across our national life. Scholars say the mass media influence our thinking and decisionmaking as individuals as well as great national or global institutions. Ordinary citizens often attribute more "power" to the mass media than do scholars who make their judgments not on limited personal observations, but on systematic study. Connections between scholars who study the media, people who actually lead and operate the media and the general public who consume the media product are rarely made. And a

---

AUTHOR'S NOTE: This essay was first delivered as a speech before the Council for Advancement and Support of Education at its annual meeting, San Antonio, Texas, July, 1986.

more precise look at "the public," persons with no apparent vested interest in knowing about or understanding media per se, reveals many knowledgeable opinion leaders in institutions ranging from the arts and business to the law and education who care very deeply about media issues and whose minds hunger for more information. In the midst of mixed views about the media — whether they are generally a positive or negative force in society — there is almost universal agreement that the media are more important than we have heretofore thought.

For many years knowledge about the mass media in all of their forms (newspapers, television, book publishing, etc.) and in all of their functions (information, opinion, entertainment, advertising) has been generated by various media professionals, critics, scholars and other commentators. This information, until recently, got little attention in the popular press or in media channels most available to the general public. And while industry leaders and professionals discussed and debated their problems it was usually behind closed doors at conventions. The scholarly community was of several minds on what is currently called media studies. In the 1930s and 1940s researchers from several fields probed and explored the media. By the 1950s for a variety of reasons that interest flagged and the torch was held mostly by communication scholars and journalism professors. The relative status and "importance" of the media, vis-à-vis other social forces, was not highly regarded. Now, that seems to have changed. There is a lively field of media studies in American universities, although its reach is still fairly limited; the media themselves are more introspective and more given to self-assessment. This has led to an active field of media criticism easily accessible to the public in newspapers, magazines and on television. Citizen leaders in various fields who have a strong interest in the media are also part of an awakening audience that is asking questions, making critical comments, and sometimes calling for action, usually legal or governmental intervention.

The woman who called me to talk about the treatment she got from CBS News wanted to know how the mass news media work, how much influence they have, how she could make personal contact and be heard, and whether she ought to file a law suit. She was a very active and attentive media consumer. In our conversation without knowing whether her grievance was justified or not, I found myself making a map as I explained how media organizations work, the relationship between a national network and local stations, the link between ownership and daily decisions, and the limited nature of public feedback.

That conversation, and others over recent years, convinced me of the importance of the need for a public dialogue between the media and the people, one that underscores the role of freedom of expression in a democratic society, but also one that realistically confronts the "manufacturing process" that brings information, entertainment, and advertising to the public.

Although we have been communicating even before early peoples made drawing on the walls of caves, the intensity of media influence in our lives has altered largely in response to changing conditions in society, whether fueled by economic upheavals, political transitions, or technological innovation. Whether we are talking about the impact of the telegraph, telephone, or television on our lives, individually or in some national collective sense, we are locating the "media variable" amid various currents and forces which the media may or may not influence and help shape. And that is the situation in the 1990s as individuals in a computer age try to cope with and confront their media.

Three great converging forces, all interrelated, are changing the shape of media in America. They are: (1) the technological revolution; (2) the economic upheaval and reconfiguration of media ownership; and (3) the resulting impact of both on the information environment and on journalistic styles and standards.

What was once in the realm of futurist forecasting is now with us. We have moved from the rhetoric of such cliches as "the age of information" and "the communication revolution" into a period when we are transmitting, processing, and receiving information with the help of microchips, satellites, and computers. We use VCRs, video discs, and on-line databases. We do our work on personal computers and subscribe to videotext services as we cope with various broadband communication systems, including cable, subscription television, and direct-broadcast satellites.

As we monitor the development of new technologies and services, their market penetration and, in some instances, their glacial growth, we also need to consider the impact that these new delivery systems are having on old media. For example, the competition for advertising dollars that these new media represent has given newspapers a much greater concern for their audiences. Indeed, as one critic said, newspapers have at last discovered the need to view their readers in a self-conscious way, something that broadcasters have done for a long time. Newspapers now engage in research and have pioneered a marketing approach to news. They are concerned more and more with market segmentation and the precise nature of their audiences.

Newspaper editors now speak not just of "the paper," but of "the product" and of "packaging," as well as the "upscale" audiences they hope to attract. Broadcasting has had more than a decade of experience with electronic news gathering (ENG), during which there has been a continued blurring of the distinction between news and entertainment. We are now experiencing a regionalization of television, in which power is no longer centralized in the networks and local stations are becoming less reliant on them. We have seen the virtual death of the documentary accompanied by the rise of mini-series and docudrama.

In the world of magazines, there is continued specialization. Indeed, more than any other medium the magazine anticipated the age of information and emphasized discrete audience segments that were identified and planned for on the basis of market research. Though they were ahead of the game, magazines now face stiff competition from other media and one another, in many instances struggling to survive. Still, magazines have always had somewhat cyclical histories; they are born, they grow up, and they sometimes die.

We need to spend more time assessing the impact of new technology (such as satellites) on old delivery systems and established media (such as newspapers) than assessing its impact on the emergence of genuinely new communication industries (relatively few to date). Remember that the time lag between the invention of a new technology and widespread use may be considerable. I think of this when I hear carping critics writing off cable television, remembering that it took 70 years for the telephone to become a truly national medium that reached 50 percent of the population. I know that technological change is rarely dramatic, but is instead subtle and incremental. As we know, the promise that cable seemed to offer in the 1960s and 1970s has not yet been fully realized. What was technologically feasible then met market and governmental resistance, and the result has been a much slower movement in that new and promising industry than we might have expected. Technological determinism is not the whole story.

The Economic Upheaval

This is a time for mergers and acquisitions, for concentration and reorganization of much of the corporate sector. This has affected the media industries profoundly. As one commentator said recently, there have been more dramatic changes in broadcasting in the last two years than in the previous 30 or 40, at least as far as ownership goes. The ABC-Capital Cities merger, General Electric's purchase of RCA (and thus NBC), and

CBS's attempt to thwart a hostile takeover bid are dramatic indicators of what is happening in the communication industry, what some have called "merger mania."

Of course, media companies make continued acquisitions: Knight-Ridder's purchase of the database Dialogue and subsequent sale of its TV stations; Rupert Murdoch's $3 billion deal with Triangle Publications in 1988; Gannett's "Triple Crown" (Des Moines, Detroit, and Louisville) in 1985 and 1986; as well as bullish moves by Times Mirror and others. Add to this the complexity of a global economy evident to media owners and entrepreneurs, and it is a turbulent and complex picture. These companies are growing, acquiring both print and broadcast properties, blurring the distinction between the print and electronic media. This is especially evident in the national editions of various newspapers, among them the *Wall Street Journal,* the *New York Times,* the *Christian Science Monitor* and, most visibly, *USA Today.* The old print and electronic distinctions are rapidly disappearing, as witnessed by the joint venture of Hearst-ABC and recent agreement between the direct-broadcast satellite service, Conus, and the Associated Press.

What is behind the economic rumbling? I believe that among other things it is a new and more sophisticated concept of marketing in the midst of great competition. Thanks to the computer, it is a discovery of audience, a recognition that there might not be a great undifferentiated national audience, or not much of one. Instead there are distinct demographic and special-interest audiences that need to be coddled and courted. This is leading to what some critics call "the death of mass communication." They argue that there is not mass communication but only segmented communication serving discrete parts of the total population. This means that there is a difference between the local "community" a newspaper or broadcast station serves, and its "actual audience;" those people who plight their troth with a given medium by subscribing, viewing, or buying advertising.

We have moved from media governed by a law of large numbers, in which the gathering together of large heterogeneous audiences served the interests of the mass media, to a law of right numbers, in which media seek smaller and more targeted audiences. What this may mean for the decline of democratization and the rise of elitism and class consciousness is a matter of much speculation. I believe there is nothing to fear, because the changes that occur in media audiences only reflect the changing nature of society and its natural segmentation into what legal scholar Anne Wells Branscomb calls "teletribes and telecommunities," new publics made possible by modern telecommunication. Beyond the traditional mass media, there are heretofore unknown audiences conversing with each other through "citizen-band" services on interactive databases.

Newspapers, still a vital force in the media community, have responded to the changing environment and economy with vigor. Faced with declining circulations and a diminishing market penetration, partly due to electronic media competition, they have commissioned market research to better understand who their audiences are. They have repackaged themselves in special sections, restructured their operations, and even encouraged new writing styles and reporting strategies. Traditional journalists decried all this, but it is very much a reality today, and not, I think, in the least harmful to freedom of expression. We have little social memory for similar upheavals in the past, including the one that brought us the mass press in the 1880s and 1890s. Then the press became more egalitarian and less elitist as it attempted to lure a new mass audience, and journalists and other critics decried that as the debasing of information. Today just the opposite is occurring, and critics are making similar charges.

The New Information Environment and Journalism

The economic pressures affecting the distribution and marketing of information have also given rise to new styles and standards of journalism. These are driven by a new definition of news that is audience-oriented and characterized by pertinence to the individual. This has led to the so-called "use paper" and to service journalism in print and broadcasting. The emphasis is on useful information in a no-nonsense age. This new definition of news has been called soft-and-sexy, humanistic, process rather than event-oriented, and many other things. It is marked by spare, lean prose that delivers useful information.

Beyond a new definition of news, there is also more descriptive, analytic reporting. Today, reporters place more emphasis on the consequences of a story than on its bare facts alone. Well beyond simple description, news today is most often in the realm of analysis and forward-looking, speculative stories. A story about a new tax bill, for example, will focus more on the effects the legislation will have on individuals than on the details of how Congress passed the bill.

Amid these substantive changes in news there seems to be a decline in investigative reporting. Perhaps this is because investigative reporting tends to run in cycles. Nevertheless there is less of it than there once was, due, many people think, to libel suits and press credibility issues. While there are still a good many investigative reports, such as journalistic accounts of Mrs.

Marcos' fortune, there is less attention given to penny ante local political corruption, diminished attention to matters involving sex and violence, except in the tabloids.

As old-fashioned, blood-and-guts investigative reporting is on the downswing, service journalism, aimed at solving people's problems and looking at the quality of life, is on the rise.

People want all kinds of information, from specialized reports on health and recreation to hard data about the economy. And, no fable, they are willing to pay for it. A magazine like the *National Journal* charges more than $600 per year for thorough, substantive reports about government. Many newsletters are pricing their subscriptions in the hundreds—some in the thousands—of dollars, while data base services charge a pretty penny for their useful wares.

We are an information society. People care about the ownership of information because more than ever before information is valuable. As keepers of some of the most credible and most reliable information in our society, we can contribute mightily to public understanding by wisely managing this great renewable resource: information that the public needs and wants.

References

Beninger, James R. 1986. *Control Revolution: Technological & Economic Origins of the Information Society*. Cambridge: Harvard University Press.

Bower, Robert T. 1985. *Changing Television Audience in America*. New York: Columbia University Press.

Dutton, William H., Jay G. Blumer, L. Kraemer, and L. Kenneth. 1986. *Wired Cities: Shaping the Future of Communications*. Boston: G.K. Hall.

Noam, Eli M. 1985. *Video Media Competition: Regulation, Economics, and Technology*. New York: Columbia University Press.

Patten, David A. 1986. *Newspapers and New Media*. White Plains: Knowledge Industry Publications.

Prichard, Peter. 1987. *Making of McPaper: The Inside Story of USA Today*. Kansas City: Andrews, McMeel & Parker.

Smith, Anthony. 1980. *Goodbye Gutenberg: The Newspaper Revolution of the 1980's*. New York: Oxford University Press.

Traber, Michael, ed. 1986. *Myth of the Information Revolution: Social and Ethical Implications of Communication Technology*. Beverly Hills: Sage.

Tunstall, Jeremy. 1986. *Communications Deregulation: The Unleashing of America's Communications Industry*. New York: Basil Blackwell.

Williams, Frederick. 1982. *Communications Revolution*. Beverly Hills: Sage.

Figure 2.1
SOURCE: Art Young, from "The Freedom of the Press," published in *The Masses*,
December 4, 1912.

2

The Media and the People

The Politics of Media Credibility

The fragile relationship between the American people and the news media has stirred much controversy in recent years, becoming a genuine public issue. While commentators and critics talk about a "confidence gap" between the public and the press, editors, broadcasters, and others worry about the consequences of this apparent disaffection. Indeed, media credibility has become something of a cottage industry with such organizations as the American Society of Newspaper Editors, the Associated Press Managing Editors Association, the American Press Institute, the Radio-Television News Directors Association, the National Association of Broadcasters, the American Association for Public Opinion Research, various state press and broadcasting associations, and others, including the Gannett Center for Media Studies launching studies or holding seminars and meetings.

Why all the consternation? One need only remember the Grenada affair when the American press was barred for a time from that Caribbean island and when public reaction was strongly anti-media. In major stories, *Time* declared "Journalism [Was] Under Fire," while *Newsweek* found "The Media in the Dock," and the *Columbia Journalism Review* asked "Does the Public Really Hate the Press?" Meanwhile several books were being written about the growing hostilities between the news media and their audiences.

AUTHOR'S NOTE: Lecture given at the Journalism Ethics Institute, Washington & Lee University, Lexington, Virginia, March, 28, 1986.

This chapter discusses the nature and scope of the media credibility crisis, as well as the media's response, and what that portends for the public. Looking beyond surface commentary, we should also consider the motivations and purposes of those who have joined the credibility debate.

Any contemporary dispute between the media and the people deserves some context. Whether it was the Grenada affair in 1983 or the attacks by Spiro Agnew on the press in 1969, it ought to be clear that the confidence-credibility-public trust question is nothing new. In earlier times, editors were lynched and newspapers torched, so the recent debate, however contentious, seems mild by comparison. I was reminded of this long legacy of press-public conflict recently at Colby College in Maine, which has a distinguished lecture series named for an alumnus, Rev. Elijah Parrish Lovejoy, who was the first martyr of the press in America. Today, there are occasional demonstrations and anchor people are sometimes hung in effigy, but nothing as drastic as those earlier expressions of public displeasure. Indeed, today, we most often learn about the dimensions and intensity of public discontent from public opinion polls, and that is exactly what happened with the present credibility crisis.

While the Grenadian affair is regarded as the trigger for the credibility controversy of the 1980s, I think it was little more than a useful indicator for some underlying problems for the press and the public. It triggered the current controversy because nothing strikes more deeply at the fire-horse instincts of the press than being barred from armed conflict. This cuts deeply into a macho mentality that goes back to the days of Richard Harding Davis and other war correspondents; additionally, it offends an article of faith for the press, that there is a legal and moral entitlement to be present where news is happening, especially when that news happens to be war. In the aftermath of Grenada, the press for a variety of reasons put itself on the public agenda and worried out loud about public distrust and hostility.

There were two principal reasons for what would be an extraordinary response by this American institution to its public relations problem. The first and most noble is freedom of expression. The press does have a mandate guaranteed by the command of the First Amendment to provide a free flow of information and opinion to a society that needs it. Any constraint on that freedom is rightly and robustly resisted. The press and its leaders worried about the long-term effects of public dissatisfaction on courts and legislatures, which so often define the limits of freedom of the press. The observation of Mr. Dooley that the Supreme Court "follows the election returns" cannot be lost on any careful observer of American life.

Beyond freedom of expression and the noble exercise thereof, was another priority for the media: money. Without stability in our marketplace economy, the press (and by that I mean individual newspapers and television stations) do not survive. These economic underpinnings were especially evident after Grenada because of slippage in the national network television audience and the continued precarious position of newspaper readership (in terms of percentage of the population that actually subscribes and thus becomes a part of the much-heralded circulation figures). In a period of economic uncertainty as new media outlets emerge, the traditional news press (especially newspapers and television news) cannot afford to take a chance that a discontented public will begin to cancel newspaper subscriptions or reduce its reliance on network television.

In this age of market segmentation and research consciousness, it is not surprising that the media and media industries responded to the credibility crisis with research. Media leaders and pollsters looked backward to an important large-scale study of public attitudes toward the media conducted in 1981 by the Public Agenda Foundation, a liberal action organization founded by Daniel Yankelovich and Cyrus Vance. The results of that study had been disturbing to anyone concerned about freedom of the press. Much of the public indicated that it did not support many of the tenets of free expression in this country and even saw the press as a barrier to their own freedom.

The Public Agenda Foundation report was one of several studies of people and the media stretching back more than 50 years, but this long-available intelligence and research legacy was mostly ignored during the next three years of discussion and debate. However, the controversy was not without some context. When asked about the apparent low standing of the press in the polls, media leaders would often say, "Yes, but look at other institutions like business or Congress or organized labor. People don't much like them either." Thus came increasing discussion of the decline of confidence in American institutions and what Seymour Martin Lipset and William Schneider called "the confidence gap," the title of their book comparing public support for and understanding of American institutions over many decades.

In the post-Grenada days, the first major organization in the field with a study of public attitudes toward the media was that of the respected American Society of Newspaper Editors, sometimes called the Brahmans of the press. In fact, the ASNE study more than anything else gave fuel to the growing controversy. It is easy to see why. Was there a credibility problem? "Yes," declared the ASNE, "a massive and major one." As the report put it: "Three-fourths of all adults have some problem with the credibility of the media, and they question newspapers just as much as they question television."

This was quite an admission for an organization whose leaders really believed that the public was mad at television, but loved and respected newspapers. But the ASNE study, conducted with scientific care by a competent public opinion research firm said otherwise. As the report put it, mention the news media to most members of the public and they talk about bias, sensationalism, invasion of privacy, and a preoccupation with bad news. This report prepared for the nation's editors (not for their critics or enemies) found a dissatisfied public concerned with the treatment of ordinary people, bothered by conflicting news reports, disturbed about the accuracy and completeness of coverage, equally disturbed by what the media covers and how it is covered, genuinely questioning the honesty and ethical standards of journalism, worried about the media as an institution and whether it was overly influenced by advertising and partial to powerful people. While a close look at the statistics often showed a close call as to whether the public was positively or negatively inclined toward the press, on a particular aspect of press coverage or reporters' behavior, the ASNE report tended (for reasons of hoped-for improvement and change) to give a less than-optimistic picture. The 1985 credibility report and one published a year later were both action-oriented with specific recommendations about how a newspaper could enhance its credibility and thus restore reader trust.

A few months later, a national study conducted by the *Los Angeles Times*, and published in that newspaper, further explored many of the same concerns raised by the ASNE report. The ASNE study was mainly an internal document, distributed to editors and covered briefly in the popular press. The *Los Angeles Times* study took the issue public and continued to stir the controversy.

The *Los Angles Times* poll was followed by a study commissioned for the Associated Press Managing Editors Association that looked at media credibility from the inside, from the point of view of editors and reporters themselves. The APME report was a study of journalists' attitudes toward credibility and aimed at bridging the gap between professional journalists and their readers. Again the APME report, like the ASNE Report conducted by MORI Research (a commercial firm), found that "nearly all journalists agreed that a high priority should be placed on improving newspaper credibility." While there was a reported rift between two groups of journalists — the "older natives" who plight their troth with a given community and newspaper and the "younger transients" who move on to other jobs—there was near universal agreement that credibility is a problem and that it is also a "serious and important issue."

Concurrent with these studies and others, we at the Gannett Center for Media Studies at Columbia University began an inquiry on the mass media and the public trust. From the beginning, we recognized that there was a long legacy of public/media consternation and that the post-Grenada flap was just the latest chapter. We were bothered that various reports rarely cited past work or noted the longstanding nature of the controversy. Thus, we invited to the table leaders of various media organizations, as well as media scholars with a special interest in the public's view of the media. Out of these discussions and subsequent field work came two studies: one, a 50-year report on public attitudes toward the news media and another, which surveyed citizens of two cities, Baltimore and Toledo, linking what people know about the news media with their attitudes and beliefs. We reported these findings at a national conference in November 1985 and also initiated the second phase of our inquiry, a study of American institutions and the news media, believing that the "blood and guts" of media credibility is found in the views of leaders of such institutions as business, the arts, the military, labor, education, and others.

Public attitudes provide one reading—a broad-based view of the general public which is made up of citizens who are not active media critics or are not personally involved in the debate over media credibility. That debate is most often led by institutional spokespersons who, in turn, are heard by and influence others. A true account of media credibility is found in a full understanding of both the public and those visible institutional leaders who speak out.

By the end of 1985, there was virtual unanimity among many, though not all, media leaders that credibility and public trust were vital issues in need of attention. The payoff, people believed, would both enhance freedom of expression and give financial reassurance to the print and electronic press.

Media credibility seemed virtually institutionalized. As we looked around at the end of 1985, we could see a seminar at the American Press Institute devoted to an intelligent and practical examination of the credibility problem, conferences at the Poynter Institute (and a subsequent book on this topic), standing committees on credibility in the ASNE and APME, and much more.

The various credibility reports signaled the complexity of the credibility problem. It was not a simple matter of taking the public temperature and counting the numbers. We knew there was a real difference between the numbers on given questions, as seen in public opinion studies, and the intensity of the noise being made by institutional leaders. We found that while the public does question most institutions, it doesn't write them off. Except for questions that focused on the constitutional role of the press and the public's understanding of freedom of expression, the public view, we thought, was mixed: neither enormously critical nor enormously supportive. But we agreed with the ASNE and APME committees that the issue was important and worthy of attention over the long haul.

In the midst of our deliberations and those of the other groups, we had been told that a major study by the Times Mirror Corporation was anticipated. Indeed, Michael Robinson, a well-known media scholar, was a party to some of our committee deliberations. The Times Mirror study was unveiled in late January 1986, first at a glittering dinner at the Plaza Hotel in New York City and the next day at the National Press Club in Washington.

On the day of the New York unveiling, a full-page ad in the *New York Times* and other newspapers hinted that the press might not have much to worry about after all, since Dan Rather (and the other TV anchors) all had greater popularity ratings than President Reagan, the most popular chief executive in recent memory. That night at the Plaza at dual podiums in the grand ballroom, Andrew Kohut, the president of the Gallup organization, and Robinson, revealed the Times Mirror credibility findings and declared bluntly that "there is no credibility crisis for the nation's news media." The report continued, "If credibility is defined as believability, then credibility is, in fact, one of the media's strongest suits." In what seemed to be a thorough and exhaustive report of high quality, the Times Mirror researchers seemed to directly contradict the ASNE findings issued only seven months earlier. Did the public have a change of heart? Were they less concerned with media credibility than all the other studies and conference reports suggested?

Philip Meyer, media scholar and former editor, had anticipated this situation months earlier in an article in *presstime* in which he warned that credibility studies needed to be read carefully. The glass might be "half empty or half full" depending on how data are interpreted, he said.

In its newspaper and magazine advertisements, the Times Mirror organization promised that its study would introduce a new (and previously ignored) factor that was important to public understanding of the press. Robinson and Kohut called this the "salience issue," and pointed out that for most Americans the news media are not all that pertinent or (as the social scientists say) salient.

How do we know? Most Americans do not sit at home at night and discuss journalists. In fact, said the study, people are more likely to talk about professional athletes, lawyers, or members of the clergy than, say, business executives, journalists or scientists. Thus, the Times Mirror study argued, if people do not talk about the media all that much, how can credibility really be a problem?

The Times Mirror study was complex, but the question remains, why the disparity? Why did ASNE declare that there was a serious credibility problem in April 1985, a diagnosis reinforced in other studies, only to have the Times Mirror put a cap on the issue in January 1986? I believe there are several plausible explanations.

Philip Meyer's observation about the half-empty, half-full glass is apt, as are media researcher Charles Whitney's observations about trend-line data over the years which indicate media credibility is long standing, but not an urgent crisis per se, unless one is especially worried about newspaper circulation or court decisions on libel. To an extent, the media are "in the dock," but they have been for long time. What is different is the relative importance of the media in society, especially in this information age which differs so markedly from the old industrial order. With information as a renewable resource and the media as purveyors of information at a time when new information services are emerging, the relationship between a specific medium and its audience is vital. So, what may seem to be somewhat predictable trends over time with some mood swings may, in fact, be a crisis for American newspapers or for network television given the contingency of the moment, the fragile economic environment, and the equally fragile climate for freedom of expression. After all, judges and juries are a part of the public and reflect to some extent public attitudes and values. A public harboring some sustained hostility or suspicion toward the press will eventually be reflected in court decisions. Some say that this already happened during the years of the Burger court, where the press got its way less often in constitutional disputes than was the case in the 1960s.

Ironically, when the Times Mirror poll was released in New York, an editor rose from the audience and asked why the report seemed to contradict the ASNE findings. The answer the editor got was that there was little real difference in the ASNE and the Times Mirror findings, but that the press misreported the original story, emphasizing the *negative* aspect of credibility. What an irony, that the press should negatively misreport a story about the press! There is something to this assessment, but only because the studies are not the stuff of either a dramatic negative (or positive) story. A better headline would have been "Newspaper Credibility: It Depends."

Given the fact that all of the studies mentioned here were of high quality, not shabby or inferior work that could be dismissed as bogus research, another explanation for the differences is found in the motivation of the organizations releasing the research: what might be called the politics of media credibility.

I confess that I do not know in precise detail the chronology of events, but the following comes close. The American Press Institute was out front early on this topic. While API does not commission this kind of research, it does run practical seminars that explore media issues for professionals from the newspaper field. In 1984 API ran a seminar on credibility and brought scholars together with media professionals to examine the growing crisis that had been signaled by Grenada. Why? Because it apparently accepted the diagnosis of public opinion polls and wanted to get editors engaged in a discussion of how any damage done to the press could be repaired by effective responses in local communities. API cares about newspapers and wants them to succeed both as citizens of their communities and as economic enterprises.

I believe that the ASNE response was also consistent with the API view and, indeed, some of the same people were involved, at least peripherally. But many ASNE members, I think, had another vested interest in separating "newspaper" from that dreaded term "the media," which includes the newspaper's nemesis, television. Some of the ASNE people I spoke with gave me the impression that they thought a study fairly conducted would show that newspapers were highly credible and that television news was not. In the unlikely eventuality such findings emerged, they would have differed sharply with studies of television as a major news source for the American people. It should be said that the people who actually conducted the study and their oversight committee, headed by David Lawrence of the *Detroit Free Press,* did not have this view. However, at least one observer has said that the researchers knew, at some level of consciousness, that a bad news report was needed in order for ASNE to have an issue worth pursuing. Not surprisingly, the ASNE report was presented with a sense of urgency to motivate editors toward self-improvement. Quite the opposite occurred, however, and ASNE was forthright in reporting the apparent rift between public and media, once again factoring themselves back into the generic term. To its credit, ASNE moved quickly to put knowledge into action, to find practical ways to make newspapers more accountable to their audiences.

APME got a later start in the credibility issue question and found much of the debate preempted by the ASNE report. Thus, with excellent professional guidance it looked inside news organizations to better understand the frayed credibility link between journalists and their readers. Again, with a somewhat different emphasis, their motive was on behalf of the institution of the press to enhance credibility for all newspapers and broadcast outlets. Nothing mysterious about this.

Public trust is a vital, enduring issue. It will not always be sexy and popular, but it will be with us as long as there are media. In probing public trust, credibility, and believability, all of us concerned with the subject were really asking, what can (or should) be done about it? These concerns led to accountability, a discussion of how the public can converse more effectively with the media, and to a more specialized, but important area, the economics of libel, something closely connected both with public trust or credibility and with accountability. For us, the credibility issue is an enduring concern, but also one that leads to other natural problems and issues for the press.

What of the Times Mirror? All that can be said for most of the other studies can be said for the Times Mirror project. The Times Mirror study conducted under corporate auspices of the parent company of the *Los Angeles Times* went into the field after the actual *Los Angeles Times* study had already been published. The *Los Angeles Times* study was conducted as a newsgathering operation and should *not* be confused with the subsequent Times Mirror report. The Times Mirror project, as a relative latecomer to research and discussion in the area, was faced with a serious problem. How to report its findings, given the likelihood that it would resemble those of ASNE and the *Los Angeles Times?* There is little public relations value in announcing to the world that "we found out what everyone else did." Times Mirror is not an academic, scholarly or professional society, but rather a corporate entity and naturally wants the corporation to get credit for public-spirited work like the credibility study. With imaginative packaging and some important additional questions that linked *knowledge about* the media to *people's attitudes*, the Times Mirror effort made a useful contribution to the understanding of media credibility. Like too many of the other reports (something true of the industry generally), there was no attempt to account for the disparity of findings of previous studies. Thus, to some, the Times Mirror effort seemed to be a "Johnny-come-lately" grandstand play to get some corporate public relations benefit for its effort. This would seem to be borne out in the Times Mirror's use of a leading public relations consultant who represented CBS and the *Boston Globe* in libel suits. This consultant has personal credibility with the media and, as one press critic told me, "When he calls and says a story is important, I usually think about covering it."

Recognizing that media organizations are not scholarly enterprises, I would still argue that a little attribution is no disgrace and that the credibility issue and other media concerns could benefit from more cooperation, rather than pronouncements of breathless reports with little context, either historical or contemporary, which, in the end, confuse and confound the public.

In conclusion, the three-year credibility debate was and continues to be a matter of useful public concern that does have very real consequences for the American people. The crisis nature of credibility will come and go as the media are put on the hotseat, but now there is considerable knowledge that can be checked and tested over time. We know more about what people do (and don't) think about the media. We know what segment of the audience (demographically sorted out) has what attitudes, both about media credibility generally and about the legal regime under which freedom of the press operates. Some of the findings are depressing; others are encouraging. All suggest the need for a dynamic process that will lead to better public understanding of the news media.

Clearly, media organizations need to explain themselves more fully, to give the public a better sense of why certain news decisions are made in a particular way. The studies also tell us a good deal about media behavior, about reporters in the field and how the public reacts to them. The studies mentioned here and others paint a picture of a public poorly informed about the news media and how they function. I doubt that efforts by media organizations alone will be adequate to address this problem.

The problem, in my view, is really one of public education. The mass media have emerged as a major American institution only in recent years. Nowhere in our educational system is there a coherent effort to introduce students to the news media, to provide not only an understanding of how the media work, but also the overarching issues of freedom of expression and its role in our constitutional scheme. People, for the most part, are not enthusiastic about freedom of the press, largely because they have never been exposed to a thoughtful explanation of the Constitution and the role of information in a democratic society. If the problem of paucity of information about the news media and press is true in elementary and secondary schools (and with rare exceptions, like the "Newspaper in Classroom" program, it is), the situation in colleges and universities is also dismal. The typical American with a college education has little exposure to systematic understanding of mass media or mass communication.

If a student does not take a course in journalism or media studies (and few outside those fields do), chances are he or she will encounter the role of the media only in courses in American government. Even so, not all students take the basic American government course. For those who do, we must ask how the media are portrayed in those courses? In an examination of more

than 30 textbooks for introductory American government courses, I found
that the media are typically presented in one of two ways: the first is the
little-effects view, based on social science research going back to the 1940s
and now considered mostly passé, that the media have only a minimal effect
on American life, whether in the political arena or with regard to consumer
behavior. The problem of media effects is one that has perplexed social
scientists for decades and is still a debatable issue, but the American government courses rarely reflect this. The other view is a *powerful press* view
mixed with a neo-Marxist critique suggesting that media are capitalistic
enterprises wherein the profit motive guides all decisions, including news.
There are precious few exceptions to these two simplistic views. And while
it is difficult to believe a student would accept the idea that television has
only a minor, peripheral role in elections, it is nonetheless a view trumpeted
in texts and in the classroom. Similarly, a Leftist polemic is not an impartial
view of the media, either.

We need media studies courses, not as cheerleaders for the media
industries, but as thoughtful commentators and guides which will give
students a survival manual for a society increasingly involved with and
enveloped by the news media. I would like to see such efforts at all levels
of the educational enterprise in America, but I would be satisfied if a few
efforts that would touch many students were organized.

The credibility crisis and the attendant organizational and scholarly efforts that grew out of it, have serious consequences. For the public, there is
a greater need to know and understand what the media are all about, how
they work and why. This can be accomplished by better coverage of media
by the media themselves and by serious efforts by the press to more effectively serve its public. For media professionals there is also a clear need to
pay greater attention to the audience, both in fashioning understandable
news reports and in defending controversial and sometimes unpopular ones.

The credibility crisis was a very great gift to the public and the media.
It should not be cursed or dismissed or allowed to drift too far from public
consciousness. The current controversy will wane and pass, but it will
return again as long as there are changing media eager to survive both as
a force for public understanding and as a commercially viable economic
enterprises.

Walter Lippmann and the American Century Revisited

There is everywhere an increasingly angry disillusionment about the press, a growing sense of being baffled and misled; and wise publishers will not pooh-pooh these omens. They might well note the history of prohibition, where a failure to work out a programme of temperance brought about an undiscriminating taboo. The regulation of the publishing business is a subtle and elusive matter, and only by an early and sympathetic effort to deal with great evils can the more sensible minds retain their control. If publishers and authors themselves do not face the fact and attempt to deal with them, some day Congress, in a fit of temper, egged on by an outraged public opinion, will operate on the press with an ax. For somehow the community must find a way of making the men who publish news accept responsibility for an honest effort not to misrepresent the facts.

The troubled and indignant words above do not come from some press pundit of today, engaging in ritual forelock-tugging at a gathering of editors and publishers, nor from some anguished target of journalistic excess seeking to warn his pursuers that they have gone too far. The concerns are highly contemporary, but they were voiced by Walter Lippmann, still the most esteemed American journalist of this century, in his 1920 collection of philosophical essays, *Liberty and the News*.

In that landmark consideration of the role the press plays in a democratic society (enjoying not just liberty per se, but liberty granted in order to accomplish useful social purposes: informing the public; serving as a forum for timely debate on the great issues) Lippmann surveyed the journalism of his time and found widespread arrogance, ignorance, disinterest in facts, and inability to engage issues. He saw a press with the extra-constitutional capacity to set the national agenda, and he saw that press squandering its moral capital on sanctimony and self-importance. He saw a populace living in a complex society, acutely in need of facts and context in order to make its own decisions in accordance with democratic principles, and he saw that populace frustrated by a lack of serious information and awash with trivia. He wrote:

Everywhere today men are conscious that they must deal with questions more intricate than any that church or school has prepared them to

---

AUTHOR'S NOTE: This article first appeared in the spring 1987 issue of the Gannett Center Journal, "The Business of News" and was co-authored with William A. Henry III and Huntington Williams.

understand. . . . And they are wondering whether government by consent can survive in a time when the manufacture of consent is an unregulated private enterprise. . . . Editors have come to believe that their highest duty is not to report but to instruct, not to print news but to save civilization.

That stern assessment was not meant to weaken endorsement for the First Amendment, nor to minimize the importance of free debate in preserving our democracy, but to enhance both. Some critics of the press, to be sure, are critics of the very notion of press freedom. But many of them — and some of the harshest come from within the ranks of the press itself — speak with affection, respect, and hope that journalism can come even closer to fulfilling its ideal role.

If Lippmann Were Writing Today

If Lippmann were writing today, after two-thirds of a century of purported progress, what would he find? Some reasons for pleasure, and some for pain. He would of course note that many more of today's journalists share a privileged education, like his at Harvard; but few of them even now have specialized academic training in law, government, the making of budgets, or the direction of private enterprise. He would find that facts and authenticity are given far greater lip service; but much of that service is paid to the potentially spurious authenticity of the electronic media (which can show and tell what was done and said, but with their extreme selectivity can mislead by omitting what was *not* done or said). He would find that journalists are not only sometimes still sanctimonious and self-important but are far more famous and influential than in his day, with the best known of them becoming much better known and more trusted than almost all of the people whom they cover.

He would find newspapers (and their electronic kin) where, more than ever, serious coverage of public affairs must compete with features on food, entertainment, sports, and "life styles," and where editors conceive of themselves as marketing directors, choosing what material to print or air based in significant measure on the audience demographics sought by the advertising department. He would find newspapers that frankly admit they do not seek — in some cases, they outright avoid — readers who lack the educational, occupational, and financial wherewithal to please advertisers. And this elitist impulse is often most visible in the very news organs that editorially call fit and proper attention to the poor, the old, the minorities, and the overlooked in our society. Lippmann would find that, in broadcasting, the editors (or news directors) have actually handed over content control to "consultants" who do not even weight journalistic responsibility except as a marketing device and who dismiss substantive coverage of government as "boring" and exploration of fundamental social issues as "a downer." Local television news would probably strike him as all too familiar, recalling the tabloid sensation-seeking of his day. He would probably be impressed by the legacy of the network TV news departments, with their traditional presence in Washington and their increased concern with news from other nations, but he would note that staffs and bureaus are being cut, coverage is being reduced, and no less a figure than Dan Rather is speculating publicly about a possibly malign shift from gathering the news to merely packaging the news.

The rapid rise of the electronic media might surprise Lippmann, although he lived to see much of the change. He would surely be troubled by the continuing confusion, not least among our lawgivers, about whether the First Amendment applies with equal force – or should – to this variety of journalism, unanticipated by the Founding Fathers. Chief Justice Warren Burger has written:

> A broadcaster has much in common with a newspaper publisher, but he is not in the same category in terms of public obligations imposed by law. A broadcaster seeks and is granted the free and exclusive use of a limited and valuable part of the public domain; when he accepts that franchise, it is burdened by enforceable public obligations. A newspaper can be operated at the whim or caprice of its owners; a broadcast station cannot.

The executive, legislative, and judicial branches have concurred in imposing on broadcasters the equal-time rule and the fairness doctrine, both of which require an even-handedness in politics that cannot be imposed on print institutions. As Federal Appeals Court Judge Skelly Wright acknowledged in a 1976 case, such treatment "does, after all, involve the Government to a significant degree in policing the content of communication."

Lippmann might have been startled to learn that in recent years courts have extended roughly the same protection to business and ideological advertising, even on purely political matters, that has traditionally been granted to journalists. The proliferation of commercial speech contributes, to be sure, to public discourse, and in the largest sense only advertising enables the mass distribution of more purely journalistic forms of speech. But to Lippmann the ability of lobbies and other self-interested groups to claim First Amendment rights clearly meant for higher purposes might sound like moral cacophony. Moreover, he would doubtless have been disheartened that the rapid growth in clearly defined First Amendment rights has far outpaced the press's self-imposed commitment to First Amendment responsibilities.

Media, Money, and Declining Voter Participation

When Lippmann surveyed the politics of his time, he found pervasive, often corrupting influence of lobbies and moneyed interests, as he categorized them

> special groups which act as extra-legal organs of government. . . . These groups conduct a continual electioneering campaign upon the unformed, exploitable mass of public opinion. . . . So politics as it is now played consists in coercing and seducing the [elected] representatives by the threat and appeal of these unofficial groups. Sometimes they are the allies, sometimes the enemies, of the party in power, but more and more they are the energy of public affairs.

Forceful as those words are, Lippmann would surely judge that the influence of organized groups in 1920 pales by comparison to their power today: a power enhanced by the highly debatable notion that limits on political contributions and campaign expenditures, particularly when coupled with public financing of major candidates, somehow constitute an attack upon free speech.

Lippmann was troubled enough by the role that organized lobbies could play in manipulating public opinion and thereby determining the direction of the debate. With explosion in the cost of campaigning (much of it spent to buy air time that broadcasters might responsibly be expected to supply free, in recompense for their free use of airwaves that still technically belong to the American people) the rise of political action committees, aptly termed "money brokers," has made electoral politics dangerously vulnerable to manipulation. In the 1986 midterm elections, Congressional candidates spent $342 million, up fully 30 percent from just two years before. Most of this money came from people promoting a legislative agenda, either to increase their income and reduce their taxes or to advance some ideological cause. These contributions are not dispensed in anything like equal proportions. One measure is that during the period 1983 - 1984, Republican Party spending at the national, state, and local levels totaled $295 million, versus $89.1 million for Democrats, a ratio that has held steady for some years; in absolute dollar terms the gap grows ever wider. But this is not a strictly partisan concern. Senator Robert Dole of Kansas, whose party benefits from this disproportion, warns, "When these political action committees give money, they expect something in return other than good government."

The fruit of this special-interest money, paid broadcast advertising, now so thoroughly dominates the electoral environment that political professionals generally refer to legitimate news coverage, debates and similar events, as "free media": a clear expression of subordinate status. Televised debates remain the principal hope for voters to form clear impressions of non-incumbent candidates who are not manipulated by image-makers or filtered through the perceptions of journalists alternately preoccupied with the horse race aspects of the election or campaigning themselves for pundit status.

It sometimes seems that debates have proliferated. Yet in the 1984 election, there were only two debates between the nominees for president, only one between the nominees for vice president. During the primary season, there were ten televised debates among the Democratic aspirants, but only two were carried on the main commercial networks and many of the others were unavailable to tens of millions of potential voters. In other races debates are still a novelty and too often they fail to serve as a real benchmark of what the candidates are saying and thinking. The coverage by the press, and even the questions during the debate, may focus instead on the strategy of timing, ground rules, and other last-minute jockeying rather than on substantive difference between the candidates.

The most disturbing development of all is the consistent and worsening drop in voter participation. Even in presidential election years, half the eligible population fails to vote, so that a "landslide" victory can be dismissed as a pseudo-mandate from little more than a quarter of the electorate. This delegitimizing of election results makes it harder and harder to attain a consensus and govern. Voter disaffection is sometimes read as a bad report card on their performance of government. One has to believe that Lippmann would have judged it, and rightly, as also a bad report card on the performance of the press.

What the Public Deserves

What public affairs information does the public deserve in a democracy? Can citizens be expected to participate if asked to engage in a sort of scavenger hunt, through overlong and undernourished "info-tainment," for serious examination of government and public issues? While congratulating ourelves on an expansion of news to a variety of sources never seen before, are we in fact being plagued with the journalistic equivalent of junk food, enjoying a binge while failing to absorb the essentials? Given that the job of the press is hard (no harder, surely, than governance, but arguably no less so) is it being performed in a fashion adequate to the task? If there is, as Lippmann argued, an essential connection between liberty and the news, is the news as we experience it promoting democratic liberty?

In an ideal world, politics itself is, like journalism, a form of education, and one of the principal aims of a political campaign is to educate the voters, so that they are better able to decide for themselves where they stand on issues and how they can best see their beliefs carried out. In the real world, of course, a great deal of politics too often turns out to be about getting elected, taking power, then rewarding the people who helped get you there. Similarly, a great deal of journalism turns out to be self-absorbed, and the invocation of the First Amendment is frequently of the press, by the press, for the press, without much reference to the genuine interests of the public.

This does not mean that the press has fallen away from its original constitutional role. Quite the contrary. The Founding Fathers intended full protection of the press's ability to deal with government officials, even in adversary ways. Having provided in the Bill of Rights for free speech for the whole citizenry, they went further and provided separately for "freedom of the press," not tentatively, not embroidered with nuances, not shrouded or bound up in conditions, but flatly and plainly. The Founding Fathers, moreover, were dealing with a press that was not only occasionally guilty of bad taste or inaccuracy but also frequently partisan, reckless, even vicious. As New York Governor Mario Cuomo has written, "Knowing all the odds, they chose to gamble on liberty."

That was, as Lippmann noted, a major step forward from the great thinkers of the ancient and recent past. In *Liberty and the News* he wrote,

> Something important about the human character was exposed by Plato when, with the spectacle of Socrates's death before him, he founded Utopia on a censorship stricter than any which exists on this heavily censored planet. . . . We are peculiarly inclined to suppress whatever impugns the security of that to which we have given our allegiance. . . . If our loyalty is turned to what exists, intolerance begins at its frontiers; if it is turned, as Plato's was, to Utopia, we shall find Utopia defended with intolerance.

Lippmann went on to cite such noted champions of liberty as John Milton, who in *Areopagitica* calls for tolerance only to add immediately, "I mean not tolerated Popery;" John Stuart Mill, whose benevolence toward any opinion diminished the closer it came to generating immediate action; and Bertrand

Russell, who wished to liberate "creative impulses" but clamp down on "possessive impulses."

Even some of our Founding Fathers and their successors have questioned whether the freedom of the press is, or ought to be, as absolute as the First Amendment holds. George Washington called the press "infamous scribblers." Thomas Jefferson, the President whom journalists most love to quote on the importance of their trade, wrote, "Even the least informed of people have learnt that nothing in a newspaper is to be believed." Theodore Roosevelt tried to bring criminal charges against a newspaper for alleging corruption in the construction of the Panama Canal. As David Anderson, professor of law at the University of Texas in Austin, has noted,

> Not until 1925 did the Supreme Court recognize the First Amendment as a limitation on the states' power to hold the press accountable. No act of Congress was ever held to violate the First Amendment until 1965. In 1919, Justice Holmes' belief that citizens could not be punished for criticizing the government was a dissenting opinion. Until 1964, libelous statements were excluded from any constitutional protection, and until 1931 local authorities could shut down a newspaper they considered malicious, scandalous and defamatory.

Countries as diverse as Sweden and Israel still require publishers to obtain a license from the government. Says Professor Anderson, "When the Israeli government designates particular subjects as secret, the press must submit articles on those subjects for prior review. Seditious libel is a crime punishable by termination of the newspaper, and truth is no defense." That is not the American way, but our openness has its price, and it is up to the press to prove, day after day, that the price continues to be worth paying.

What ought journalists to do? To begin with, they ought to re-read Lippmann. They ought to turn to the Hutchins Commission report of the 1940s, *A Free and Responsible Press*. They ought to ponder anew the lessons that are professed to have been learned at nearly every conclave of their confraternity. And then, instead of demonstrating humility and sincerity in words, they ought to demonstrate those very real qualities in action—before and during, rather than after, the fact.

As a general principle, journalists must acknowledge that the public's oft-cited right to know includes the right to know, in detail, about both logistics and the philosophy of coverage they will read, hear, or see. Some hard-liners still believe that, as W. P. Hamilton of the *Wall Street Journal* argued in years gone by, "A newspaper is a private enterprise owing nothing whatever to the public, which grants it no franchise. It is therefore affected with no public interest. It is emphatically the property of the owner, who is selling a manufactured product at his own risk."

Other, more enlightened media executives believe that they make themselves accountable simply by competing in the marketplace. But as John C. Merrill, professor of journalism and philosophy at Louisiana State University, has argued,

> The main problem is that, in the real world, the 'people' are largely passive or unconcerned about the routine affairs of the media. Feedback of any significant kind — is episodic and splintered. It offers little or no real guidance for media policies. The media, we can say, are dependent in a capitalistic society on the marketplace for financial support, but relatively unaffected so far as professional and moral guidance is concerned. . . . The only logical accountability system or model is self-accountability, based primarily on a self-imposed foundation of ethics or morality.

The basic goals of such self-regulation are unexceptionable: to ensure fair and honest reporting, to provide reconsideration of instances when reportage may have been dishonest or unfair, to provide a platform for divergent opinion or analysis from both prominent and ordinary citizens, and to open lines of communication between the editorship and the readership. Yet such codes are notoriously difficult to enforce: The first act of the American Society of Newspaper Editors when it was founded in the 1920s was to write a code of ethics, yet the organization promptly found itself spending five years debating whether to compromise editorial autonomy and censure a member who had clearly violated the code by involving himself in the Teapot Dome scandal. The vote might come a little sooner today, but the outlines of the debate would be pretty much the same.

News Media and the 1988 Elections

Fortunately, the press has a ready alternative to negative or self-castigating discussion. As the nation enters the 1988 Presidential campaign (surely the most important matter that journalists will cover day–to–day), why not make that coverage a case study of responsible, accountable journalism? Given the integral and, by its own evaluation, frequently counter-productive role that the press often plays in campaigns, why not use this great public event as an opportunity to engage in ongoing, public self-assessment, and disclosure?

What can the press do?

First, it can give its audience, the American people, a dance card or blueprint, defining intentions about the scope and coverage of the campaign, explaining as far in advance as possible what resources will be committed and on what basis the choices about whom and what to cover will be made. Of course those judgments will change over time. But advance disclosure will require the press to be more honest with its constituency, and with itself, about what underlying values and principles are shaping its allocation of money and manpower.

Second, it can explain what those resources consist of: the budgets, the reporters and their backgrounds, and the space or air time they can command. The moment to set aside time for debates, for example, is now. So is the moment to commit a page or two in the newspaper, or five minutes once or twice a week on the nightly news, to a straightforward summary of what each candidate is saying.

Third, and here the mandate becomes more complex, the press can resolve to be more than a mere transmission system for politicians, institutions, and special interests. Lippmann worried about an insufficiency of facts. Modern editors must worry about a failure to distinguish, or at least set priorities, among a flood tide of data, and must disprove the old adage that their calling is to cull the wheat from the chaff and then publish the chaff. Editors can define early and publicly what issues are important to the public and can systematically confront candidates with probing questions, refusing to accept evasion or mere rhetoric. In 1986, for example, many candidates chose not to speak out on homelessness, or AIDS, on the need for new taxes or for protective tariffs. Some of these matters were clearly on the minds of the public; others were concerns shared privately by nearly every responsible official in Washington. Journalists are always talking about keeping control of the agenda, about making campaigns more substantive and about giving voters a more clear idea of who the office-seekers are. Stating the issues and hammering away at them can allow the public to judge both the relevance and fairness of the coverage and also the caliber of the candidates. Although ours is a nation that in the end votes for the person, not the party or sometimes even the philosophy, knowing where the candidates stand — if they do in fact stand up to be counted — is the best way to come to understand their true character. And if the candidates believe that one or more of the media are emphasizing the wrong issues, having to take a clear stand will provide them with a full opportunity to make a counter-case.

Fourth, the press can clearly chart and disclose where campaign monies come from, how they are spent, who may be seeking what kinds of influence, and whether the marketing strategies of particular candidates may ignore or effectively disenfranchise certain kinds of voters. The press, especially the broadcast press, cannot be expected to be hostile toward the hands that feed it, nor should it be. The same First Amendment rights that give us a free flow of ideas have been interpreted to allow individuals, including candidates, virtually unlimited spending to promote their own ideas or, via slight subterfuges, those of people whom they support. The use of PACs and of so-called soft money (nominally channeled to the parties but really on behalf of particular candidates and vested interests) is not technically illegal and must be treated with due diligence. But following the money trail, however complex, is an essential part of the story and must be told early and often. In this instance the often over-aggressive press may actually be too polite, even timid.

Fifth, the press, especially the networks, can conduct during the course of the election the sort of self-analysis that is generally left to postmortems. It is said that political journalists, like generals in the French army of the 19th century, are always prepared to fight the last battle. That is probably the case, because the forums and their queries should commend close attention. Even during a canonization, after all, the devil's advocate gets his due. And these forums should not be polite and neutral. As former White House Counselor Lloyd Cutler has said,

> Every profession has a tendency not to speak ill of its brethren. I would think that one of the things the press could do best is to expose the weaknesses of its fellow members, as A.J. Liebling did so well. What has happened to the A.J. Lieblings? Where are they today?

Where, in particular, are they during campaigns? One place they are is banging on the door seeking entry. There are few enough press critics as it is. Their effectiveness is greatly reduced by the notorious disinclination of journalists to submit to the same freewheeling questioning that they impose on news subjects.

Sixth, journalists should hold candidates accountable to debate; and despite the lure of glory, reporters should stay clear to allow those meetings to be real debates rather than heavily orchestrated press conferences. Let the candidates engage each other, challenge each other, catch each other making mistakes. If both sides misstate the truth or sidestep major issues, the press will have plenty of opportunity to point that out, and the voters just may have noticed already, anyway.

Much of this behavior would simply improve the press's performance in the role it already plays. But some would serve the at least equally valuable purpose of having the press explain, to its public and to itself, just what its place is in national life. Is it a de facto branch of government by virtue of its special legal rights? Is it a part of the system of checks and balances, serving as an informal brake on the other branches? To what extent does it, too, "represent" the people, and to what extent should its coverage be expected to be "representative"? Whatever the answers, and they will differ from institution to institution, certainly from journalist to journalist, the very process should serve as an antidote to detachment and arrogance. Indeed, this process of accountability may help remind journalists that their goal must be to educate the public rather than, as often happens, themselves, and that their primary purpose is to provide information rather than insight. As Lippmann said in 1920, and could easily judge of today, "We must go back of our opinions to the neutral facts for unity and refreshment of spirit. To deny this is to claim that the mass of men is impervious to education. In terms of public opinions, this means a resumption of the contact between beliefs and realities which we have been steadily losing since the small-town democracy was absorbed into the Great Society."

American Media and American Values

Whether American media shape, contribute to, reinforce, detract from, or are irrelevant to American values is a worthy topic. This is especially true given the ubiquitous nature of the mass media, which have become a kind of central nervous system for the nation and, perhaps, the world. Discussing media values and American values takes on a different character today than it might have a decade or two ago. As we have witnessed the diminished influence of the family, the school, the church, and the political party, the media take on a larger role in our personal and national lives.

The importance of the media is reflected in our strong feelings about them. I doubt there is anyone who does not have an opinion about the way television and newspapers deal with Presidential elections. And it would take little prodding to elicit from most people a personal reaction to their local newspaper, the CBS Evening News, or *Time* magazine. Clearly, our media touch us as individuals as they deliver information, entertainment, sports, advertising, and much, much more.

Everyone these days is exposed to and conditioned by media from a quite early age. For me, growing up on the Oregon coast, my earliest memories of media were of the *Oregon Journal*, our local weekly newspaper, the Portland radio stations, and a radio station in the next town. Television came late to what was then called a "fringe area," so it was these older media that commanded my interest. The *Journal* was especially important. I read it voraciously and it was a special link with the outside world. *The Oregon Journal* was a liberal, pro-labor paper whose masthead included a bald eagle with a streamer in its claws bearing the old territorial motto: "She flies with her own wings." Anchored on the editorial page above letters to the editor were the words of Voltaire: "I disapprove of what you say, but I will defend to the death your right to say it." Strong value statements to be sure.

The *Journal* gave its readers, even young readers, a lot. I got a pen pal from New Zealand through a column in the youth page, which was called "*Oregon Journal* Juniors." That page and the people who put it together were a kind of youth club which encouraged children to write letters, collect stamps and coins, and pay attention to world affairs. And I recall the dramatic headlines over Drew Pearson's accusatory columns that demanded morality in government. As a youthful reader in the 1950s I was getting a dose of values. Nowhere did these values come to the fore with more vigor

---

AUTHOR'S NOTE: Lecture presented at "Forum '87: In Search of American Values," Reed College, Portland, Oregon, October 15, 1987.

than in the comics. Nothing conveys judgmental views more dramatically than the comics, as they plead for special interests. There were the ultra-conservative mutterings of "Little Orphan Annie," the militaristic promotions of "Steve Canyon," and the social-work ethic of "Mary Worth." For me these early encounters with media encouraged independence of thought and mind, egalitarianism, freedom of expression, internationalism, conservation, and much more. Of course, most everyone has had similar experiences as we learned to use and live with media. Today young people rely on television programming, MTV, comic books, and video games, all of which bring to them a view of the world outside their immediate surroundings. And, most assuredly, all of these media have messages that express values.

The media are so deeply integrated into other institutions that we actually depend on them. The values media promote join in chorus with each other. But does that chorus blend harmoniously with the views of most Americans or is it discordant and abrupt?

To understand the intricate relationship between American media and American values, we must first understand them both. Historian Henry Steele Commager says we Americans are self-assured people who feel good about our own power and success. Our culture is predominantly material; our thinking quantitative. Our genius is inventive, experimental, and practical. We are also careless, good natured, casual, generous, and extravagant. We cherish individualism, but are also conformists. We believe in order, but distrust authority. And above all, we profess faith in democracy, equality, and liberty. In a survey of the dominant personal and social values of American society, two sociologists, James Christianson and Choon Yang, rank ordered American values. This is how Americans expressed their preferences:

1. Moral integrity (honesty)
2. Personal freedom
3. Patriotism
4. Work (your job)
5. Being practical and efficient
6. Political democracy
7. Helping others
8. Achievement (getting ahead)
9. National progress
10. Material comfort
11. Leisure (recreation)
12. Equality (racial)

13. Individualism (non–conformity)
14. Equali:y (sexual)

Other scholars concur, suggesting that most major dilemmas in our society center on values, whether we are talking about the views of a Supreme Court justice or the character of a presidential candidate. Always, we return to activism and hard work, achievement, efficiency, materialism, progress, freedom, individualism, equality, morality, humanitarianism, and nonconformity as core values of the American people, which are sometimes contradictory, sometimes in harmony with the values of the media.

Consider the lively exchange in the White House Rose Garden in 1987. After a ceremony honoring educators, President Reagan passed by Sam Donaldson of ABC News who asked whether the nomination of controversial judge Robert Bork to the Supreme Court would be withdrawn. Even before the President responded (his answer: "Over my dead body!"), some of the teachers yelled, "Shut up!" Amid hissing and booing, there was an angry exchange between the teachers and the reporters present. "You ruined the ceremony," said one of the teachers. One added, "We're disappointed with you, Mr. Donaldson!" While another said, "We teach our students that all rights have responsibilities." Donaldson snarled angrily back at the teachers, saying he was disappointed they did not understand freedom of the press and the role of the White House press corps. Clearly, there was a clash of values. The teachers preferred a polite ceremony without the irreverent questions from the Fourth Estate. The reporters thought they had observed protocol, holding their questions until the President was finished with the ceremony. This was a clear disagreement. Were the news media simply carrying out their constitutional and workaday functions? Or did the reporter go beyond the bounds of propriety?

The media not only reiterate and reinforce American values, but they also teach morals as they preside over a communication system that binds our society together. This does not mean the media would win a plebiscite on any particular social or political issue. But, cumulatively, they lead, reflect, and reinforce American values more often than they depart from them. I realize this is not the intent of reporters or editors who consciously try to produce impartial work, but it is an inevitable result, largely because the media by default do what family or school might have in the past. Systematic knowledge about mass communication is still too uncertain to give precise calibrations about the relative impact and influence of the media on individuals and society. However, accumulated evidence, especially in the last 20 years, tells us that the media make an important imprint on people, affecting cognitive choices and thus on institutions and culture. Of course, media have a near monopoly on information about public affairs, business, culture, sports, and other topics. Without the media, we would not communicate very well, if at all. And, the media do seem to "set the agenda." That is, they make choices and decide that one issue, event or person is more important than another. Hence, some activities get attention, some do not. Does this mean the media tell people what to think? No, but scholars and commentators agree that the media do tell us what to think about as they narrow and refine the focus of public discussion.

As we know, most American media must first be commercially successful to function at all. Second, because American media are the only businesses specifically protected by the Constitution, they have a special obligation to provide a flow of information and opinion to the citizenry. The media give us information or news; opinion, usually expressed in editorials; entertainment and advertising. The social scientist Harold Lasswell said these services deserved a loftier formulation. To him, the functions of media were:

1. surveillance of the environment;
2. correlation of the parts of society responding to the environment; and
3. transmission of the social heritage from one generation to another.

To these has been added entertainment, since the media help us celebrate each other, our institutions, and life itself. The media also serve as change agents, assessing and explaining society's contours, whether they are incremental or wrenchingly radical. But functions only reflect the values of the institution and its mission. They are not themselves values. The values most important to media (if their content and staff behavior are any indication) include immediacy, accuracy, fairness and balance, intelligent interpretation, diverse opinions, and so on.

Are the media moral teachers and enforcers of a social code? It is understood that few in the news media seriously think of themselves as arbiters of taste or monitors of American values. Still, when Ted Koppel asks Al Campanis about racism in the major league baseball or when the *Miami Herald* investigates Gary Hart's private life, the media are doing journalistic work that also happens to have strong and value-laden morals. Cumulatively, then, the media call on politicians, business leaders, and others to account for their public (and sometimes private) performance, holding them up to certain standards.

Some scholars argue there are certain ideal "end states" or "terminal values" which allow us to be individually and institutionally happy, secure, free, and, perhaps, even wise. The media do not traffic in these long term visions. But, the road to these goals requires something the media can provide: so-called "instrumental values," which require an ample supply of ambition, broad-mindedness, forgiveness, honesty, intelligence, responsibility, and other high-minded characteristics. It is the juxtaposition of these instrumental values that become tools in the quest for terminal values, ideals which can never be fully achieved, of course.

In such a scheme, several Presidential candidates in the 1988 campaign stumbled as they professed a highly moral, long-term vision for American society. Their private lives and apparent character failed to meet their own tests. Thus, the media became vessels for the virtuous society. In this role the media can be high-minded critics, moral arbiters, common scolds, or mean-spirited investigators.

Because the media wield ever increasing power, we do need to worry about their institutional values because the stakes are so high. We should also care about the people who work for the media — their outlooks, personal values and ethics — because the media are becoming quasi-public institutions. We depend on the media for all manner of human transactions, from our buying habits to politics. This makes it imperative for all citizens to know these omnipresent but poorly understood social institutions.

When we ask what values are embedded in media organizations, we find they are not so different from those elsewhere in society with one important exception. The media see themselves as part of a system of freedom of expression. Freedom of the press is a fundamental liberty linked closely to several of the preeminent American values mentioned earlier. To journalists, freedom of the press has an almost religious character and is clearly "the preferred freedom."

Journalists profess strong opposition to corruption or conflict of interest. They are suspicious of power of all kinds, except possibly their own, which they discount and denigrate. They say they strongly favor equal opportunity and oppose racism and sexism. Their politics are slightly liberal, although one critic recently called them "the best and the blandest" since few journalists are really very ideological.

We should remember, though, that journalists are not like most other Americans: they are better educated, make more money, and have more defined social and political views. They are also more likely to be single, to live in an apartment, and are less inclined toward religion. Reporters and other media people are really members of an elite. They are not Everyman or Everywoman and thus are not likely to hold the same values as their white- and blue-collar neighbors. Due to these differences, some media enterprises fail economically: in other instances, they were bombarded by critics. The rub, of course, is that sometimes courageous news organizations are appropriately "out of touch" with their communities. The paper or TV station that takes on the local leadership or public opinion and stands against deeply-held but wrongheaded community values, may actually express the most American of values while breaking with the "roar of the crowd." However, most media organizations that are out of sync with their audience are not courageous crusaders, but inattentive and insensitive to audience needs and interests. They can benefit by the market research, readership studies and electronic rating services that give them information on which they can act — or not — depending on the circumstances.

I doubt that market research is enough to keep media values and American values in harmony. Still, there is a need for a social safety valve wherein people can talk back to the news media. Letters to the editor columns, and complaint files at broadcast stations are not really an adequate remedy for this very real social need. In fact, the trend toward deregulation across society means that a large portion, possibly the majority of electronic messages, now reaching the American people are not governed by the language of the Federal Communications Act, which commands that electronic media operate in the "public interest, convenience, and necessity."

New technologies outside the rules of the FCC and the impact of deregulation are responsible for a veering away from the public trust. There is no definitive answer for this, although many feedback approaches have been proposed and most have failed. Several community-media councils wherein complaints from the public are adjudicated have not been a hit. Some of the earliest work of this kind in the United States occurred in Bend, Oregon with the support of Robert Chandler, a respected publisher. That experiment died quietly a few years ago. A National News Council effort failed in 1984 and only the Minnesota News Council still functions. Metropolitan press councils in cities like Seattle and Honolulu were brave experiments. Perhaps it was the quasi-judicial nature of the press councils that doomed them. I do not know, but I do know that means for feedback wherein community people and media people meet and discuss issues and grievances are healthy and important for democracy.

Similarly, television badly needs a feedback mechanism for citizen's grievances. The letters at the end of *60 Minutes* are not enough. The British have developed a program formula that works there. It should be explored in the United States, where television and its people deserve understanding and support.

Clearly, the press ought to do a better job covering itself, but that prospect is somewhat bleak both because there seems to be no compelling reason for media organizations to do it, and also because, in the end, this would result in a conflict of interest where the press would assess and evaluate itself and we could rightly ask, "who will guard the guards."

Perhaps the best solution would be a dedicated citizen or academic effort, one that does not yet reflect the deep split between press people and the rest of us. And their work, largely routine, would be aimed at communicating with the audience, rather than being a forum for their own views.

Occasionally the press finds itself as "odd man out" while much of the rest of the citizenry takes sides with the President. To them, the press had no business "intruding" on that little war in the Caribbean and the press asked rhetorically, "Why do they hate us out there?" The credibility of the media has slipped a notch or two in the last 10 years, a factor closely watched by leaders of the media and other institutions.

While most people do believe what they read and see — something not true, for example, in the Soviet Union, South Africa, Chile, and a few other countries — there is more to credibility than believability. Thus, dissatisfaction and distrust of the press is high when compared with other American institutions, such as government and business.

Some critics argue that in a system like ours, market forces will correct disparities, and to some extent that is the case. We do have choices, different standards and styles of journalism, that reflect different values and appeal to different outlooks and views.

Consider the different assumptions of these four types of journalism:

1. *Public affairs reporting* assumes that coverage of politics and government is preeminent, deserving surveillance and consistent monitoring. The result tends to accentuate the negative and it is often argued that public affairs journalism emphasizes the seamy side of American life. Look to most daily papers and network television news for this form of journalism.

2. *Problem-solution journalism* tends also to be slightly negative; this kind of journalism is seen most dramatically in the *Christian Science Monitor* and various urban weeklies. It looks at the world as a series of problems (public or private), which can be corrected with alternative solutions. This journalistic approach is useful whether it focuses on economics or on prenatal care.

3. *Descriptive-analytic journalism* is found daily in *The Wall Street Journal*, which delivers long stories that include description, detailed ex-

planation, and evolution. Usually there is a human interest angle and a link to large humanistic problems.

4. *Marketing approach journalism,* which brought us special sections in daily newspapers, is linked to market research, and carefully courts (or panders to) public taste. Local television news, with its reliance on ratings, is the best example here. *USA Today* champions this genre with its "journalism of hope."

As you can see, all of these styles express and reflect different values. And, in fact, you will find aspects of them in the output of most news organizations.

Essentially, American values and media values are not far apart, but there is real potential for a serious rift. There have been cases when a newspaper or TV station was out of sync with its audience and community. Sometimes it would seem in the public interest to create a high-tech hotline wherein people's comments about the media — "the good, the bad and the ugly," in the words of Col. Oliver North — could be inventoried and sorted out. I would not propose a system of arbitration or adjudication, but rather an inventory that would be given to media organizations and other concerned institutions such as business, the arts, or education. The media and their critics could decide what, if anything, to do with this information. Perhaps organize a public forum. Perhaps encourage the public schools to teach more about the media in the context of American history or social problems. And the media themselves might respond.

If they learned that most viewers did not understand a particular newscast, this would be helpful to the television news staff. If an editorial was perceived as biased and unfair, that might tell the editorial writers that their writing was not very compelling. Most of the problems and issues raised would not be the stuff of libel suits, but would help solve workaday problems and misunderstandings. But those are the issues that, in the end, inspire trust or foster suspicion in the media. Perhaps then, American media would better reflect the people they serve and also contribute to public discourse. This would give leadership and offer the public the kind of information and intelligence that they deserve.

We do depend on our media to be stewards for values and for moral purpose. And, if that is to be the case in this era when the family and the school are not as effective as they might be, we Americans are entitled to a better system of feedback because healthy communication between any institution and its public requires an open channel whereby true conversation ensues.

The Press as Moral Teacher, I and II

I. Few people in the news media think of themselves as moral teachers or for that matter as managers of enterprises that bind our society together.

In a cumulative sense, the media call on politicians, business leaders, and others to account for their public (and sometimes private) performance, holding them up to certain moral standards. Social scientists argue that there are ideal "end states" or "terminal values" wherein we are individually and institutionally happy, secure, free, and perhaps even wise. Behavior on the road to such "terminal values" requires, in the sociologist's term, "instrumental values," with an ample supply of ambition, broad-mindedness, forgiveness, honesty, intelligence, responsibility, and other high-minded characteristics.

Thus, in such a scheme, we know that a presidential candidate's short-term behavior might not comport with his (or our) long-term vision for American society. Pointing out such deficiencies is often the task of the news media in an election year and at other times as well. That the media should engage in such a social enterprise as part of its newsgathering function is appropriate, of course, even though there are potential problems when any institution becomes a vessel for the virtuous society. Media critics try to keep the press honest by turning a critical spotlight on inconsistencies in the communication industry's record on matters ranging from the employment of women and minorities to nepotism and cronyism, the same kinds of flaws that the media identify in their scrutiny of public affairs. Yet all too often the media quickly pass this over, accepting their own good intentions on such matters and paying little attention to their actual performance.

So in 1988 while Ted Koppel asked a baseball executive about minorities in leadership roles in professional baseball, little was said about minorities in network television. Some argue that the public really is not interested in media issues, that such intra-industry shop talk will bore readers and viewers. Still, when pushed on it, press leaders reluctantly say that their internal practices are more important to the welfare of the nation than those of professional sports. Yet sports issues get far more attention than media issues.

In the late 1980s a suit involving black employees of the New York *Daily News* did bring the minority employment issue to light, but the reaction of

---

AUTHOR'S NOTE: These essays first appeared in *Communique*, the newsletter of the Gannett Center for Media Studies.

some media leaders was curious: They said the case might make some editors and publishers *less* likely to hire minorities for fear of litigation. Had baseball's leaders offered such a rationalization, they would have been roundly attacked in the media for their insensitivity and hostility to change. Here there seems to be one standard for the media and another for baseball, as well as other fields.

When it comes to personal morality, the media also have a mixed record. There are a few highly publicized cases wherein media people were chastised for violating a personal or moral code, as with the publisher of the *Arizona Republic* in 1987, and there are other examples where reporters' conflicts of interest are scored by media critics. The values the media profess and the values that govern media executives and employees may or may not be the same. It is hard to tell. Without accepted codes of ethics or genuinely shared values, no one really knows what the rules are.

But we ought to think more and more deeply about whether the values that benefit society at large should apply to the media both in their public activities as well as to internal operations.

Just as important is the cumulative effect of media values on American values. The media in all their functions — informing, entertaining, editorializing, advertising — command a greater and more sustained audience than the other players, namely education and religion, that are generally acknowledged to be ours and society's moral teachers.

It is not enough for the media to think only about their short-term role in monitoring vice and virtue in American society, but also to consider long-term cumulative effects of what they are doing and saying. This requires a broad societal view and a willingness to look inside their own organizations, perhaps even to allow others to join in such a social audit.

Critics and citizens alike ought to ask such questions as, what would the media have individual citizens and their own leaders do? What values do editorial voices promote? What values permeate the corporate cultures of the communications industry? What values do media leaders express, both in short-run pronouncements and long-term performance? And what of media education? Does it play a special role in a world where both the news and the nickel must coexist?

Such great issues as media credibility and, by extension, accountability, are vital to our theory of democracy.

For while the media set high standards that embrace the best instincts of humankind, at the same time they must themselves be open to public scrutiny.

II. Plagiarism is not typically a topic that makes news, but it was the central factor in Senator Joseph Biden's decision to withdraw from the 1988 presidential race. Biden's injudicious borrowing from the campaign speeches of Neil Kinnock of the British Labor Party and further revelations about his law school record were covered extensively by the media and brought about the downfall of his candidacy.

Discussions of plagiarism, usually confined to the teachers' lounge or student disciplinary councils, suddenly occupied a larger canvas as it was regarded a matter of public consequence. Biden's apparent plagiarism, commentators said, reflected badly on his character and his credibility.

The case which seemed minor with the passing of time, nevertheless, raises again questions about the role of the press as the public's unelected representative and scrutinizer of the values of candidates for public office. Few argue that the press should not have published the embarrassing similarities between the speeches of Mr. Biden and Mr. Kinnock, but the intensity of the coverage was widely questioned.

Why, some asked, is the press paying so much attention to the embellishments and misrepresentations of Biden, which seemed in any cosmic sense to be small matters? Why haven't other candidates (and several presidents) who have exaggerated their accomplishments and misstated their views gotten similar savage treatment? With what intensity should the press focus on issues of this kind to the exclusion of other news? And why did there seem to be new standards in the 1988 election campaign?

The last question may be the easiest, since the long reach of modern technology makes the juxtaposition of old and new videotapes quite simple, and, perhaps, because there is a new moralistic mood in the country.

The other questions are part of the window through which the media look at candidates. If the ideal presidential candidate is three parts statesman, two parts executive and manager, one part public affairs officer and one part teacher, it is also assumed that this ideal candidate will be trustworthy, credible, and a person of outstanding character. While one learns relatively little about the intelligence, not to mention the decision-making capacity of the candidates, we do learn about their personalities, public presence, and character. While people and events make news, deeper issues, including more complex moral ones, rarely make headlines.

Once again, the "glass-house-and-stones" maxim emerges, for while every school child is taught not to plagiarize, it is a bit disingenuous for the media to trumpet the evils of plagiarism without considering the condition of their own houses.

While appropriate attribution is an essential ingredient in good journalism, it is not uncommon for the press to copy wholesale, without giving credit, ideas, formats, graphics, and writing styles from their competitors. It is quite rare for news organizations to lift substantial passages outright, although that, too, has been known to happen.

From *New York Magazine's* "Ten Worst Judges in New York" to the *USA Today* weather map, copycats in the media readily appropriate one another's work. For years some major papers borrowed freely from others, whether specific news and information or makeup and design, without even a nod to the originator of the idea or concept. Similarly, terms like the "reindustrialization of America," taken wholesale from the writings of sociologists, are appropriated by politicians and eventually reach the public on the cover of newsmagazines. The implication is always that the media invented the term.

If the content of the media is subject to such transference, so are its visual and graphic images. It is not uncommon for the networks to share, borrow, and steal from one another. The same is true with local television and radio stations. In an age where information is increasingly regarded as property, this sometimes creates problems and results in litigation.

In a few instances, such borrowing is undergoing change. Today, it is not entirely unusual for a newspaper or television network to cite a source, even when it is a competitor, when covering a story or pursuing an idea somebody else had first.

The point is that if plagiarism — even benign plagiarism — is bad for politicians and public officials, it is also bad for the media. In this era of renewed interest in ethics and morals of all kinds, the mass media should look carefully at themselves as they scrutinize others. The media's longstanding opposition to the stuffy attribution of the academy, footnotes and all, might benefit from some reassessment.

The Press as Representative of the People: At What Cost?

May it please the Constitution.

As a student of the press and the law, I am especially interested in the fragile and perplexing interaction between these two great institutional forces. I believe they are best understood in the words of Yogi Berra's son, Dale, who, when asked to compare himself with his father, said, "Our similarities are different."

Constitutional rights are often explored with great eloquence, but much less intellectual energy is directed toward the corollary of rights, that is, duties or responsibilities.

Those who care deeply about the role of mass media in American society speak more often of *rights* than of *duties*. There are frequent conferences, workshops, and symposia to explore the rights of journalists and broadcasters, media institutions themselves, and even the public. While some commentators have tried to critically assess the *duties* of the press, they have often been rebuffed by First Amendment absolutists who argue that nowhere in the Constitution does it say anything about the responsibility of the press to do or be anything in particular.

This is true enough. But nowhere in the Constitution is there an explicit guarantee for the media to attend public trials, have access to public records or public meetings, or a myriad of rights and privileges that have been deemed permissible by court interpretations of that short, negative command of the First Amendment "that Congress shall make no law abridging freedom of speech or of the press."

The spare language of the press clause of the First Amendment has been supplemented mightily since 1791, and particularly in this century, with statutes, court decisions, and various agency regulations. They have come to constitute a complex corpus of mass communication law that must live within the general boundaries of our seemingly boundless law.

The expanding definition of press rights has been subject to much scrutiny, especially in the face of the growing influence and power of mass communication, which often has more immediate impact on public life and public policy than some of our more venerable representative institutions like the Congress. Witness the demise of Senator Gary Hart's presidential campaign in 1987 and 1988, wherein the principal players were the candidate and

---

AUTHOR'S NOTE: Speech given at the Ninth International Smithsonian Symposium, "Constitutional Roots, Rights and Responsibilities," commemorating 200 years of the American Constitution, May 21, 1987, Washington, D.C.

the press. Neither government agencies, the Congress, nor the courts played any role at all. Nowhere in our Constitution are we given any specific instruction about how the media should cope with situations like this one.

The steady expansion of press law, which has paralleled the monumental growth in the influence of the mass media, has taken the concept of "the Fourth Estate" well beyond Fourth of July rhetoric and made it a reality in today's Constitutional scheme. Some scholars, and even I, argue that the press is a legally sanctioned "representative of the people," that it acts as surrogate, trustee, and "official mapmaker" for the public. Some recent Supreme Court cases actually describe the news media as "the necessary representative of the people." The judiciary and legislative bodies have extended more and more privileges to the press that are not routinely available to the public. Some have decried this kind of "First Amendment exceptionalism." But it nevertheless is a fact of life.

The many explicit rights and privileges extended to the press in recent years have had relatively few strings attached. Still, some press victories have been greeted with uncritical applause by the media without much consideration for the subtle constraints that they may eventually place on our freedoms. *New York Times v. Sullivan*, the great case that all but abolished the law of libel as applied to public officials, is an example. Originally hailed as a monumental press victory, the lessons and explicit text of the case laid the groundwork upon which later rulings challenged various processes and procedures the media use to gather, process, and disseminate information. Law professor Alexander Bickel's warning that "the more we define freedom, the less freedom we have," seems to be the operative lesson here.

This lesson should not be quickly passed over. In an empirical study of all media cases heard by the Supreme Court since 1789, it was determined that the media had less success in the Supreme Court than most other classes of litigants. The study, carried out by Professor David Anderson of the University of Texas School of Law while he was a fellow at the Gannett Center for Media Studies, is a stern warning for media organizations who, with little thought, support bad causes through appeals or *amicus* briefs that, in the end, help only the lawyers who write them, certainly not the press or the public. Media litigants, Professor Anderson learned, seek and apparently get Supreme Court review much more often than their adversaries, which is ironic because as a class they generally do worse than other petitioners. Knee-jerk litigation strategies in the name of the First Amendment may, in fact, be weakening our Constitutional freedoms.

Through the years, the development of rights that apply to the media (and often to the public generally) have stimulated thinkers to consider more fully the role, purpose, and responsibilities of the media as a quasi-public institution. From Walter Lippmann's seminal writings giving theoretical foundation to liberty and the press to Robert Maynard Hutchins' Commission on Freedom of the Press, which posited notions of a press both free and responsible, Americans have grappled with the idea of media accountability.

There are two commonly cited models of media accountability that *seem* to work effectively. Both are imperfect and problematic. One is the economic marketplace, which, based loosely on John Milton's notion of truth prevailing over falsehood, posits that irresponsible communication will not meet the market test, that it will alienate the public, and will eventually have a negative impact on the press as an institution. Critics cite the life-and-death cycle of our media to document this case. But, there is little good evidence that individuals can very effectively "vote" with their subscriptions or Nielson ratings in an effort to talk back to the news media. The other model is litigation. People who are displeased with the behavior of the press can sue, and they do it with increasing frequency and at great economic costs.

Efforts by citizens groups to critique the press, such as voluntary press councils and fair trial-free press committees, have had limited success and have affected few people. Similarly, the various media ombudsmen who are employed by the press as in-house critics can still hold their national convention on a single bus, so small are their numbers. Moreover, self-imposed codes of ethics rarely are rigorously enforced by the media organizations that promulgate them.

The nexus of public opinion and the press has gotten considerable attention of late, most recently after the *Miami Herald's* 1987 revelations about Gary Hart. Well before that, though, media organizations devoted considerable private attention, public handwringing, and even self-congratulation to their standing in public polls. Several industry, professional, and academic groups fretted publicly about their credibility, worrying that as much as 75 percent of the American public think they are not credible. When measured along several dimensions, the media do not fare very well, even when compared with other unpopular institutions.

On the other hand, the Times Mirror surveys of recent years (which, by the way, simply equate credibility with believability) bring happier news. They suggest that network television anchors are more popular than the President — even at the height of President Reagan's popularity — and that the media are generally well-respected. But even the Times Mirror's sanguine surveys have a darker side, indicating that the best-educated and most accomplished citizens are also the most vehement and negative critics of the press. This is not a healthy situation for an institution whose authority in our democratic scheme is largely linked to credibility.

More generalized public attitude studies of the press, and there have been scores of them over the past 50 years, seem unconnected to reality in the face of the Gary Hart case. The public, polls tell us, thoroughly disapproved of the behavior of the *Miami Herald*, while really not questioning the right of the *Herald*, or anyone else for that matter, to cover the candidate and publish its findings in a timely way. Here the ethical and legal dimensions of media rights overlap and differ, pointing out the "differences in their similarities." The press, presumably, has the law on its side. While there can always be a post hoc review, courtesy of the courts, the Hart campaign is now history, and any damages, if indeed they could be proved, would be a Pyrrhic victory.

Many press spokespersons, from the Penny Press editors of the 19th century to contemporary media leaders, have made the case for *vox populi*, suggesting that the people are the press. That means, in part, that the press acts on behalf of the people and presumably that is what the press does in covering campaigns and elections. That does not mean the actions of this "Burkean" representative always please the people in either the short run or long run. But in some cumulative sense, it is necessary to have credibility in order to have authority, even in public communication.

Thus the press tampers with a fragile relationship, that of its public franchise, when it takes on any controversial subject. And today, more than ever, it exposes its methods and manner of coverage to the public. The media are thus held accountable in the court of public opinion, if not in the courts of law; what media are held accountable for is the completeness of their work, for the professionalism of their people, and for their commitment to public service, which is, after all, the rationale for press privileges under our Constitution.

Studies showing that the press is not particularly popular point up a cyclical phenomenon. What is more bothersome and far more threatening are those studies that indicate the public might not believe as strongly as the press does in freedom of the press. In fact, there are those who believe that the press clause of the First Amendment would not survive if another Constitutional Convention were called.

With this in mind, the American media could create a vision of a responsible press by engaging the public in a vital fashion. Specifically, they could use the 1988 presidential elections as a self-conscious case study, demonstrating to the public what responsible and newsworthy news coverage of this great public affair is all about. They could do this by considering the following recommendations in this or any election year:

First, they can give the American people a *blueprint* of the coverage they plan for the campaign, explaining whom and what they will cover and why. While those judgments may change, delineating them in advance would force the press to address the principles that underlie its coverage.

Second, they can explain what resources they bring to the task, from their reporters to their news budgets. This would foster understanding of how those resources are used to give regular, straightforward accounts of what candidates are saying and doing.

Third, the press should endeavor to be more than a mere transmission belt for politicians, parties, or special interests. Instead, they must define early and publicly what issues are important, and then confront the candidates with them, refusing to accept evasion or vague rhetoric. If persistent in this effort, the press will allow the public to judge the relevance and fairness of its coverage while assessing the integrity of the candidates. And if candidates believe the media are focusing on the wrong issues, they can clearly demonstrate this — thereby improving the public debate.

Fourth, the press should follow the money trail that winds through all candidates' campaigns and says so much about who influences them, who gets left out, and what the money buys. This is an important part of the campaign story that all too frequently is underplayed.

Fifth, the press — and particularly network TV news — should periodically critique its own campaign coverage during the course of an election, rather than waiting until it is over, which does considerably little good and leaves any lessons for another campaign still far away. Such self-examination would be particularly useful if it included the candidates and their staffs, whose voices should be heard.

Finally, journalists should stay clear of the spotlight during debates, allowing candidates to debate one another rather than following the dictates of what has become essentially an elaborate press conference.

If the press were to attempt this kind of coverage, we could more effectively answer the question of whether it is functioning as an effective "representative of the people." It would tell us whether the benefits of a competent and concerned press, that on occasion causes embarrassment to individuals, outweighs any painful liabilities.

After all, a free press ought to be the linchpin in our Constitutional faith, not an instrument to undermine other freedoms or to cause more harm than good to the public weal. We ought to remember that the pieces of our Constitution, and especially the enumerated rights, are there because they advance and elevate democracy. The press generally does that, although there are times when it comes dangerously close to tearing the seamless web.

References

Adler, Renata. 1986. *Reckless Disregard: Westmoreland v. CBS et al.: Sharon v. Time.* New York: Alfred A. Knopf.

Benjamin, Burton. 1988. *Fair Play: CBS, General Westmoreland, and How a Television Documentary Went Wrong.* New York: Harper & Row.

Bezanson, Randall P., Gilbert Cranberg, and John Soloski. 1987. *Libel Law and the Press: Myth and Reality.* New York: Free/Press Macmillan.

Commission on Freedom of the Press. 1947. *Free and Responsible Press: A General Report on Mass Communication: Newspapers, Radio, Motion Pictures, Magazines, and Books.* Chicago: University of Chicago Press.

Dennis, Everette E. and Eli M. Noam. 1989. *The Cost of Libel.* New York: Columbia University Press.

Fry, Don. *Believing the News.* 1985. St. Petersburg, FL: Poynter Institute for Media Studies.

Isaacs, Norman E. 1986. *Untended Gates: The Mismanaged Press.* New York: Columbia University Press.

Whitney, D. Charles. 1985. *American's Experience with the News Media: A Fifty-Year Review.* New York: Gannett Center for Media Studies.

"You might as well knock it off, boys. Nielsen reports <u>nobody</u> is watching."

Figure 3.1
SOURCE: Drawing by Opie; ©1970. The New Yorker Magazine, Inc.

3

The Changing Economics of News

The best way to "know" journalism is both through practical experience and formal study. There are dual lessons of knowledge and experience in this time of great economic change for the news media.

The impact of the changing economics of news and democracy in this, the 200th anniversary year of the Constitution of the United States, confronts us in many ways. We see it when CBS makes budget cuts in its news division or when a television station in Texas asks the FCC whether it can drop its local news programming.

In television, we are conscious of economics and democracy when the battle between networks and local stations creates news programming that some network people have characterized as "Scott and Tiffany Go to the Summit," in which two blow-dried local anchors do mindless commentary from the scene of great world events, courtesy of satellite transmission. Change is also evident when daily newspapers develop special sections and talk about "upscale audiences" and "positioning their advertising for demographic advantage." These are indicators or artifacts of change in a period of economic crisis for the news media.

But we should remember that a crisis is not a catastrophe. Rather it is a time of great change. At such a time we must ask whether advertising—the presumed culprit—really has a profound effect on news decisions and whether news is an economic commodity for sale. We must also ask

AUTHOR'S NOTE: Speech given at the University of Arizona Department of Journalism on the occasion of the dedication of the Harold O. Love Reading Room, February 12, 1987.

whether these factors are new or part of a long and enduring tradition in American journalism.

Competition is the hallmark of the media's present economic crisis. In broadcasting, the networks and local stations do battle with cable and other emerging technologies that have taken away part of their traditional audience, a phenomenon that has caused a historic drop in advertising rates. Competition also marks the fierce battles between daily newspapers and advertising shoppers for the same readers, as well as the forays by competitive newspapers into one another's cities and counties, territory that had previously been off-limits.

As you can see, what we are often talking about is the relationship between news and advertising. I am not suggesting that advertising directly affects the content of the news in any nefarious or conspiratorial fashion or that advertisers control what reporters write and editors edit. Not at all.

But what is happening now is an effort to make the news pertinent to the audience so that it attracts readers and viewers who advertisers want to reach. The notion of news as a "profit center" offends many people who care about television news. But perhaps it should not, because news has always been a profit center in the print media and I do not believe that fact has compromised its integrity.

After all, news is what people pay for when they subscribe to a newspaper. In the early days of the American press there was a mix of news and advertising, with ads even appearing on the front pages of the little broadsheets that were the forerunners of modern newspapers. In time, with the rise of professionalism, news and advertising were separated. Each took on a distinct identity and purpose, and their relationship became more circumscribed.

Scholars note that in the early days of the Republic, Benjamin Franklin personally participated in all of the then available communication activity. He could, and had, personally set type, written stories and composed broadsheets as well as sold advertising and delivered papers. Today we live in a world of specialization, where people rarely cross the lines between different functions and jobs, let alone different media. One aspect of that separation is the notion that news and advertising, while interrelated, should not intrude on each other's territory. Of course there are egregious exceptions where this separation of functions has not been observed. So, although *news* has always been a profit center in the print media, a commodity for sale, professionalism has been a major force in curtailing the commingling of journalism and advertising.

The broadcast media are another story. Over the years news has been a less dominant element than entertainment, which actually paid the freight for public affairs programming. There were reasons for this. From the early days of radio, broadcasting has been a regulated medium with government licenses and a more limited First Amendment mandate. News was thought not to have a bottom-line profit-and- loss role in the equation. Instead, news was part of the public trust or public interest purpose of broadcasting and therefore somewhat immune, at least in theory, to the pressures of the marketplace.

Broadcast news grew up in a "Golden Age" when Edward R. Murrow and his "boys" wrote the book on professionalism and impartial, quality coverage. They infused broadcast journalism with the spirit of the First Amendment which, courts say, commands the media to provide a free flow of information and opinion to the people. News was a sort of loss leader for broadcasting— not yet a profit center.

Then came the revolution wrought by *60 Minutes,* CBS's superb public affairs program. At once news was not only profitable but *highly* profitable, and the rules of the economic marketplace came into play. Still, broadcasting of radio news and television news lived somewhere between government regulation on the one hand and the commercial marketplace on the other.

With the profit motive entering both network and the local television markets, the idea of news as a commodity, so well imbued in newspapers, came to broadcasting.

All this has happened in a world of heavy competition. It has been aided by the substantial deregulation of broadcasting and other telecommunication. Such deregulation has relaxed content doctrine standards and allowed for different patterns of station ownership. Add to this the impact of new technologies, and the result has been the rise of market segmentation for the media. The advertising people in the media, with the help of advertising agencies, gather data to demonstrate the audience characteristics of a particular medium and its desirability as an advertising vehicle. They sell this idea to advertisers, and the result is a fierce search not for the *total* audience but for the *right* audience.

Indeed, these changing economic contours of American media have been described as a substantial shift from a *law of large numbers* to a *law of right numbers*; instead of courting the largest possible audience (the biggest numbers), there is more of an effort to reach specific readers and viewers, those who are typically well-educated, well-paid, and destined to spend money on the advertiser's products. Advertising departments of the media manage this activity, and thus influence the way the editorial side "packages" its product. Again, this is not by any means a direct interference with the news, but a desire to produce a newspaper or telecast that is commercially viable. Where there was once a more pronounced separation of news and advertising, there is now much more commingling between the money people and the editorial people in the media. Even some of our greatest national newspapers invite the circulation manager to the morning news huddle, once a place where only editorial purists discussed the news of the day.

The shift from large numbers to right numbers was at first more evident in newspapers than in broadcasting. Newspapers suffering from circulation declines and the death of their afternoon editions began to package themselves more attractively, with special sections aimed at specific readers. Designed to arrest the decline of circulation, the new sections also led to some reorganization of staff and the inclusion of new content, much of it of a soft news or feature variety.

Television and radio still court the mass audience, although they, too, look carefully at the demographics of their viewers and listeners. They have not typically lopped off viewers as readily as newspapers have abandoned readers by raising their subscription prices. Still, they are vigilant in trying to hold onto large audiences, even employing gimmicks and glitz. The result has been the "entertainmentization" of news, which began with "happy talk" newscasters and has continued with super graphic pyrotechnics as well as stylish anchor people.

In an era when some critics say the *mass* media are dying and that only demographically-defined and targeted media will survive, television news is facing fundamental change. Recently, and for the first time in its history, network television lost part of its audience share. The reason: Where there were once only three or four channel choices in a local community, now thanks to cable, there may be 40 or more. Obviously greater choices diffuse the audience and hurt the Big Three national networks. Add to this VCR use, and the drain on the old, stable network audience is understandable. This brought down advertising rates and led to some of the present upheaval. Also, partly because of deregulation, the networks have undergone the most significant ownership changes in their history: CBS changed management and refinanced itself; ABC became part of Capital Cities; and NBC's parent company, RCA, was acquired by General Electric. The result is true economic upheaval that portends profound change for the news business.

To ascertain what these changes mean to *news*, it is necessary to look carefully at *individual* media.

In a nutshell, it seems to me that in spite of their changes *newspapers* are improving and enhancing their news work. There is now better specialty reporting, such as business and economics coverage, and a better attempt to humanize complex stories about government finance, in terms that are meaningful to readers. There are strong and weak papers, some that are doing serious work and improving news gathering and some that are not. In the main, I am encouraged by the changes that have come to the newspaper and think that, generally, the public benefits from them.

Television news is another story. The networks still have high-caliber news divisions, able to deliver detailed content on a wide variety of public affairs subjects. And within limited time constraints they do a good job. Local stations have a mixed record. Some offer first-class public affairs reporting in major markets; however, an increasing number of local stations deliver the electronic equivalent of tabloid journalism: sleazy headlines and stories that emphasize violence, sex, and crime. They often pander to morbid curiosity and contribute little to public understanding.

Radio news is a disaster if we are to believe recent comments from the Radio and Television News Directors Association. Radio news, once nurtured and propped up by the Federal Communications Commission, fell victim to deregulation, which has caused many stations either to curtail their news operations drastically or drop them altogether. The public, I believe, is badly served by this trend.

Magazines that deliver news, including the newsmagazines and several business and specialty magazines, are a bright spot on the news front. They are competing for the audience and, generally speaking, are offering more news with depth and analysis than they once did. Some newsmagazines once known for their heavy-breathing prose have cleaned up their act and are now exemplars of serious reporting. They are facing tough times, though, as competition for advertising dollars intensifies and as structural reorganization is brought on by an era of lean-and-mean management.

Thus the state of news in America today is complex and conditional. Overall, however, I think there is enough slippage, especially among the largest audiences, to be concerned.

If this is the case, we need to ask what concrete steps can be taken to improve the news and better serve the public affairs needs of the American people. Several come to mind:

First, we need the media to do a better job of covering themselves: we need strong media criticism and reporting on media issues and events. Local newspapers should report on and analyze their news competitors: print and broadcast; television should do the same.

Second, journalism and communication schools should be much more vigorous as scholars and critics of the media. They may wish to "adopt a group" and do a serious examination of a particular media organization, as publisher James Ottaway, Jr. has suggested, or perhaps do "reciprocal criticism," as Ben Bagdikian has proposed. In the first scenario, every journalism school in the country would do serious study and analysis of the reportorial performance of a given newspaper group. Cumulatively, such efforts across the country would provide valuable information to improve and upgrade journalism, embarrass those engaged in questionable practices, and offer constructive suggestions. The second scenario would, for example, have the journalism schools of Arizona examine the press of New Mexico, while New Mexico's journalism schools studied Arizona's press. This method, it has been argued somewhat factiously, would discourage any punitive impulses by media executives and owners, not to mention state legislatures.

Third, news people need better pay and more professional development. Even industry figures gathered by the American Society of Newspaper Editors and the Radio and Television News Directors Association suggest that American journalists are badly underpaid when compared with professionals doing creative work in other fields. Indeed, at newspapers with circulations under 100,000, beginning reporters are paid less than entry-level school teachers. More staff development and management training are also important in this equation.

Fourth, we need more formal feedback between the media and the public. Here television has been especially unresponsive. I cannot believe that American television, with its great talent, financial might, and massive audiences, cannot find a commercially viable method of facilitating public discussion of television.

Finally, serious consideration should be given to regional and state press councils, possibly modeled after the pioneering and important Minnesota News Council, which has strong support from that state's media and still provides a safety valve for the public. Professional societies, press clubs, journalism schools, and others concerned with the news media should lead these efforts and enlist the help of public-spirited citizens who believe that better public affairs information is important to democracy itself.

Therefore I hope that we as citizens who honor the First Amendment will use this bicentennial year and the period between 1987 and 1991, when we will celebrate the birthday of the Bill of Rights, to reassert the meaning of a free press and remind the media of their obligation and their duty to provide news and information of importance and value to the public.

The World Outside

It is something of a truism to say that this is a time of great, even wrenching, change for America's media and media managers. Truism or not, it is vital that we understand fully the massive economic, technological, and legal-regulatory changes we are living through. This period is marked by much economic upheaval that sometimes results in dislocation of people and organizations that make up the communication industry. Sometimes, unfortunately, our media managers and, yes, our educators, act as though this were not the case.

With this in mind, I would like to advance some reasons why we need to:

* pay greater attention to "the world outside" our own enterprises and activities, on which we are normally fixated;
* understand the natural propensity for isolation, insularity, and even parochialism in each of the media industries and among their managers;
* be aware of the emergence of a new professionalism, a whole-institution model that disputes the unnatural separation of business and editorial elements in print and broadcast media; and,
* find a systematic way to get ahead of the curve by improving the education and training opportunities for media professionals who aspire to management positions.

Much has happened in the 25-odd years since Marshall McLuhan first spoke of the communication revolution, the information society, and the global village. These terms, once buzz words that conjured up images of a distant, electronic future, now aptly describe our world with its computers, microprocessors, satellites, and other technological devices. The prediction that we would become an information or communication society wherein the information sector would out-distance the legacy of the industrial revolution—the manufacturing and extractive industries, not to mention the old agrarian economy—is now with us. And Daniel Bell's prediction that we would know the information society when more than half of our people were regularly engaged in jobs involving the "manipulation of symbols" has also occurred.

In this new information society, with its great promise for information prosperity, there has also been information poverty. For some, the new technology enhances life; for others, it imprisons or enslaves. The point is

AUTHOR'S NOTE: Speech given at the Poynter Institute for Media Studies, St. Petersburg, Florida, July 1987.

WINTER 1989

GANNETT CENTER
Journal

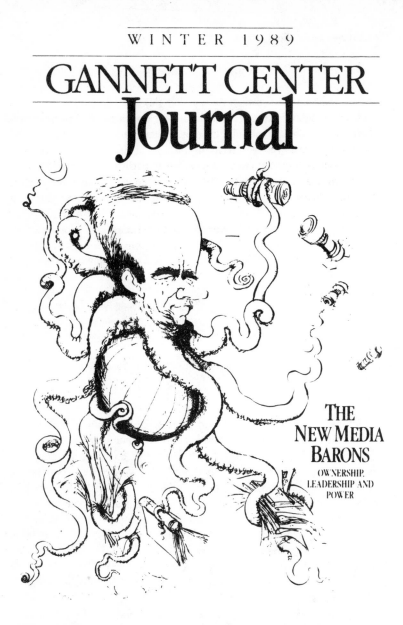

THE
NEW MEDIA
BARONS
OWNERSHIP,
LEADERSHIP AND
POWER

Figure 3.2 Artist Ronald Searle's rendition of Rupert Murdoch's increasing control over communications properties worldwide.
SOURCE: *Gannett Center Journal,* Gannett Center for Media Studies. Used by permission.

that there have been some surprises in this new information society, some of them entirely unexpected. While the information sector has grown steadily, there have also been shakeouts. We have seen the number of computer companies expand, then decline. And, closer to home in the media family, there has been both a continuing decline in the number of newspapers and a continuing concentration of ownership.

In broadcasting, the once-mighty and impenetrable networks have experienced major ownership shifts. If you do not think there has been profound change in broadcasting, just ask the hundreds of people once happily ensconced at CBS who no longer have jobs. It was once said that the TV networks were three pipelines to the American people for information and entertainment. When there were only three pipelines, it made good sense to be in the *pipeline business*. But now, as more pipelines develop, it makes sense to be in the *oil business*, and the networks are not in the oil business, at least, not yet!

The problem most notable today for the national networks, and to some extent, at local television stations, and most assuredly for newsmagazines, is a mad scramble for readers and viewers. There is one great audience made up of many parts with many suitors among the media family. Newspapers, of course, are part of this mix too, but they showed more foresight than these other media in their planning and research in the 1970s. By necessity they corrected some of their most serious problems, which then involved a diminishing readership. Newspapers accepted market segmentation, leaving behind forever the notion that they are instruments of mass communication aimed at everyone. Network television has yet to learn that lesson.

The force shaping the changes I have mentioned is, of course, the economics of mass communication, which has seen new players. Among them are cable systems and VCRs, free-circulation newspapers, more aggressive big-city dailies and suburban papers, economically vigorous local television stations that can circumvent network services with their own satellites, and much more. The new media have given us a more demographically complex audience. Naturally, there are questions about which medium delivers the most appropriate audience for which advertiser. Not incidentally, this has contributed to a soft and shifting advertising market.

All of our media institutions have also experienced technological change, wherein new time-saving machines have changed the individual's role in the workplace, the structure of management, and the nature of the product itself. These economic and technological shifts have been accompanied by deregulation of the communication (and other) industries as well as new legal interpretations in courts and legislatures of what media can and cannot do.

If we stand back from this dynamic and breathtaking scene we see the realization of John Wicklein's wise prediction that all forms of communication will come together in one "electronically-based, computer-driven system." Communication is communication, and the old barriers between and among media, their people and profits, are more blurred than ever before.

The emergence of the information society and its meaning in everyday life were recognized early on by many players: lawyers and bankers, major media companies, the advertising industry and, perhaps most importantly, by Wall Street. Even if some media executives were too busy to understand what the information society would portend, clearly others did.

If top leaders of the media industries and various institutional investors recognized that we were quickly becoming "one world" in a media sense, not everyone else did. In recent months I have witnessed these (and other) examples of a parochialism that ignores the information society:

Item: Three distinguished newspaper editors object to an appearance by Peter Jennings in the starring role at the annual convention of the American Society of Newspaper Editors, saying "We should have had a real journalist [e.g., one of us] up there."

Item: A newspaper industry association in the Pacific Northwest announces that it will evaluate, rate, and reward journalism schools in its region strictly on the basis of their dedication to the interests of newspapers.

Item: A leading advertising executive laments that yuppie media buyers in his agency do not read newspapers, even though they are responsible for placing advertising in all media.

Item: A former network president says he never thought direct-broadcast satellites would have an impact on local TV stations and their relationships with the networks.

Item: A young advertising account executive laments that he cannot get his peers interested in media industry trends because there is no incentive for them to know anything not immediately pertinent to their specific jobs.

Item: A newspaper editor proudly comments that he never watches television news and hasn't ventured inside a TV station in 10 years.

These are curious artifacts in an era when the communication revolution has created an information society marked by interrelationships and interdependence of media. Still, at a time of change, people resist and avoid the shifting environment around them, even in their own field. If it was once quite common and acceptable for media managers to be single-mindedly dedicated only to their own enterprise, that is fast changing. A newspaper editor who does not understand the public's use of television, or the advertising executive who knows media only from audience studies, are anachronisms. There is, of course, a natural Luddite tendency to decry change. In my experience of studying news practices of newspapers and television stations, I have encountered a number of editors and news directors who steadfastly deny that their definition of news has changed in the last 10 years, even when confronted with empirical evidence to the contrary.

The media, like other business enterprises, are quite transitional. New technology that works mechanically and electronically is put in place without proper management backup or understanding. New sections are added to newspapers without understanding that they stand for different concepts of news, requiring new staffing patterns and sometimes even different writing styles. These and other examples are only symptoms of the great transition between an industrial society and an information society.

There is no reason to think this transition will occur either naturally or smoothly. Well beyond the resistance to change and the unsettling nature of being challenged to do things differently, it should also be said that media organizations do little to formally prepare or train their people for such change once hired. With few exceptions, they typically rely on other institutions—journalism schools, mid-career programs (of which there are few)—and personal initiative for education and training. Change, of course, comes in many forms, and for at least 50 years the changes that beset print and broadcast media were gradual, hardly noticeable.

Now that is no longer true. From ownership changes to internal restructuring with new roles for individuals, the media industries are lively places with new expectations about the future, immediate and long-term.

In some fields, notably law and the sciences, the world of practice can look to the academy for leadership and "cutting edge" ideas. This is rarely true in journalism education, which tends to follow rather than lead the media.

Social and institutional change naturally have an impact on the people who run the media enterprises—on executives, managers, and their employees. They also have an influence on the very nature of professionalism as we now define it. The debate over whether journalism is a profession, or a craft and calling, is older than any of us. It dates from the period when ideas of professional education were sweeping the nation in the wake of the Flexner Report of the Carnegie Foundation, which was credited with reforming medical education.

The U.S. Labor Department, for political reasons, long ago defined reporting and editing as "nonprofessional activity." In recent years, that standard has been reviewed in the courts at least twice: first in the *Concord Monitor* case and currently in the *Washington Post* case. Unfortunately, from a rational point of view it is regrettable that the issue has been reduced strictly to a wage-and-hour dispute when the obvious need for a truly professional designation would clearly benefit industry and society. I hope these legal and economic issues will be resolved and that the journalistic function will take its rightful place as a professional activity that meets Flexner's criteria as effectively as any other profession, except possibly the clergy. Flexner's standards required that:

1. The activity consists of intellectual operations coupled with large individual responsibilities;
2. raw materials of the work are drawn from science and learning;
3. the learning is practically applied;
4. the technique is communicable by education;
5. there is a tendency toward self-organizing;
6. practitioners are increasingly altruistic.

When professionalism has been discussed in the media context, it has almost always been confined to editorial employees and has rarely extended to the business side. Editors were professionals under this theory; publishers and advertising directors were not. This bifurcation had its roots in the assumption "that the ethics of journalism and business are in conflict and that journalists must organize to protect themselves against the spirit of the counting room," wrote J. Edward Gerald in his seminal 1963 book, *The Social Responsibility of the Press.* Gerald was one of the first scholars to extend the definition of media professionalism in his call for the "whole-institution model." He maintained that the old separation model made little sense and ignored the real issues of power and control.

Thus he found much more attractive the idea that: ". . . the whole institution—business and communication combined—should undertake professionalism, [a concept which] accepts the unity of communicators and their business partners, rather than seeking to make them opponents within the same firm. The whole-institution proposal offers the best opportunity for long-run success."

In championing professionalism throughout the media organization, complete with advanced education for all managers and key employees, Gerald was scorned by the press and by fellow educators. The *Chicago*

Tribune offered a nasty rebuke, arguing that it was absurd to think one could professionalize the business-side of the press.

Now such leading industry figures as Robert Marbut of Harte-Hanks proudly display their graduate training in business. Editor Michael Fancher of the *Seattle Times* has urged his editorial colleagues to see business operations as something other than filthy lucre. Instead, he says, they should become first-rate managers and draw on MBA training. As strategic planning in media companies has become more common, the unity of the whole-institution model has become more acceptable. Diplomatic relations between the two "sides" is common, and the professionalization of all white-collar media personnel seems appropriate. Studies of media ethics, which have usually only traced the behavior of editorial employees, have recently, in the work of Philip Meyer and others, been linked to publishers as well.

Certainly business-editorial cooperation has been enhanced in recent years without treading on basic values. The idea of total separation always had a fantasy-land quality, and the new approach is merely the practical realization of the importance of all players in the media organization. This does not mean that editorial people do not fight conflicts of interest or separate economic values from news values, but it does mean that there can be collaboration and unity of purpose. After all, media must reach an audience in order to survive. To do so they must exercise both commercial and public trust functions, all of which should be governed by a high standard of personal conduct and overall organizational behavior. Still, in our commercial media, only an effective and profitable business allows ultimately for survival. When Henry Luce offered the axiom (roughly paraphrased), "first the nickel, then the news," this is what he was talking about.

As the new professionalism emerges, there will be difficult conflicts. This is especially true when nonmedia owners take over media enterprises. This is exactly what happened at two of the major broadcasting networks in the last two years. Hotel and insurance magnate Laurence Tisch became chief executive officer of CBS Inc., and General Electric bought RCA, which owns NBC. It was at NBC where corporate values collided dramatically with media values.

In what he thought was an innocuous memo, NBC president Robert Wright, formerly head of the General Electric Credit Corporation, called on all NBC employees to contribute to Political Action Committees (PACS). The idea of people in a media company — except for the owners — contributing to partisan political campaigns was repugnant, especially to the NBC

News division. Mr. Wright soon learned that his subordinates were willing to go public to decry his action. The lesson was that the business of media may have most of the essential characteristics of other businesses, but in some respects the media are different. Their public trust function and franchise under the Constitution set them apart and makes some activities outside the acceptable limits of institutional behavior.

The new professionalism has not yet been fully defined; it is emerging in the executive offices of media companies and filtering down to people who work in television stations, newspapers, magazines and other enterprises. It embodies the idea that the whole institution requires highly educated and trained personnel, all of them professional. It means mutual respect and appropriate collaboration to produce the newspaper or television program. It does not mean a mixing of functions, but instead a close working relationship where purely economic considerations and purely journalistic matters keep their distance.

We should ask how we can ensure that media managers and students of media management, new professionals with business and editorial instincts, can be in touch with their field, their industry, and the environment outside in order to avoid insularity. I have several recommendations, some of which depart from present industry practice and patterns. They include:

Support media management courses and programs within the schools of journalism and communication, but not to the exclusion of liberal learning generally. This should be done in the context of a systematic understanding of media-society relationships. For the most part, I believe, this work should be at the graduate level, although some material tailored for undergraduates can pique their interest and lead them from specific industry problems to more general issues.

Encourage reform in journalism education. The journalism schools have not yet caught up with the information society, let alone placed themselves in position to provide leadership. "Business as usual" in the journalism schools, clinging to the outdated ideas and practices of the 1940s, will not serve well the industry or society.

Urge the media to do more of their own training. In-house education, issues-oriented seminars, and other activities that foster professional growth and development must be initiated in order to avoid a generation of Luddites incapable of responding to the modern world. The media industries lag behind other fields in this regard and need to catch up. They cannot expect the relatively few mid-career programs or the journalism schools to serve their quite specific and idiosyncratic needs.

Communicate regularly with mid-career programs, professional-development efforts, media think–tanks and other institutions, urging them to be responsive to vital industry and society needs.

Read widely, broadly, and across the several media fields. At the moment the trade and professional magazines are most useful. Several academic and quasi-academic journals are also of value. Monitoring this new knowledge and information has to be calculated, since few media professionals have an immediate incentive to be well- informed. Increasingly, though, the broadly informed person will lead media enterprises while narrow specialists will be relegated to limited venues. .

Engage in and provide funding for research about the media and media issues. There is a world beyond practice, involving thoughtful analysis and systematic scholarship. Without it, the media will not cope well in an era when research and development chart the future.

Taken together, I believe these recommendations will provide a channel toward more useful and more intelligent media, led and managed by people with professional values and a commitment to communication as a lifelong pursuit, aware of the special place they play in all of our lives.

News, Advertising, and the Public

Although Thomas Jefferson once complained that "advertisements contain the only truth to be relied on in a newspaper," it has long been an article of faith for the American news media that advertisers should not directly influence news coverage.

Indeed, when contrary evidence turns up, the media and the public alike call it unethical journalism, not worthy of public trust. While it is generally agreed — and both recent and longstanding inquiries confirm this — that advertisers do not dictate the news and that the news media do not pander to advertisers in deciding what to cover, there is, of course, a necessary symbiotic relationship between these two great forces that fuel our commercial media.

In the United States, news is and has always been a commodity for sale. From the colonial press to the present, advertisers have paid to reach the people who bought newspapers for news of commerce and public life.

Some people would agree with Jefferson that advertising itself has informational value. For newspapers and news magazines, advertising has played a commanding role in the production of revenues. For them the news is, of course, a profit center. Whether it should be has rarely been discussed or debated, since with rare exceptions the editorial and advertising ends have kept their distance, thus preserving the integrity of the news. However, the shape and content of the news has changed and shifted over the years as new formats, graphic presentations, and even writing styles have changed.

As audience tastes changed, so did the news. With every change has come comment and controversy. The development of the wire services ended a tradition of long, discursive essays, bringing instead short, clipped reports.

Joseph Pulitzer, now venerated as a patron saint of journalism, was regarded as sleazy in his own day when he transformed the New York *World* from a paper with heady intellectual content to one with the breezier journalism of public affairs. The same debate arose when, in the 1970s, American newspapers repackaged themselves and editors began to speak of "the paper" as "the product."

What we are seeing today, of course, is part of a continuing scramble for an infinitely complex and growing audience that is being courted by a variety of media. Network television, the news magazines, and others compete for some of the same advertising revenues.

AUTHOR'S NOTE: This essay first appeared in the April 1987 issue of *Communique*, the newsletter of the Gannett Center for Media Studies.

Although broadcast news comes from a different tradition than print, that is, it was regulated by the government and expected to serve the public interest, defined in part as delivering news of public affairs, and was not actually a profit center until recently, it does live in the same competitive world with other media.

The relationship between news and advertising, between the public trust functions of the media and the profit motive, is at the heart of much of the present controversy over television news and newsmagazine predicaments. The age of information has brought with it much upheaval and dislocation — most of it unexpected.

Only a few years ago, social commentators were predicting that the communication industries had infinitely bright prospects, that social dislocation would more likely occur on assembly lines in Detroit. The prospects are still bright — as the audience expands and revenues accelerate — but there are also more media outlets and a fierce competition for audience in an age of segmentation, forcing many of our media to change, not incrementally as in the past, but with dispatch.

Nielsens, Noise, and Numbers

The American media consumer has been strangely absent this summer from the controversies about audience research that have erupted in the pages of the industry trade press. At first glance it might seem unreasonable to expect the public to care at all about the research methods and practices that monitor their viewing, listening, and reading patterns, but in recent years the battles between and among various researchers and research firms have reached a high pitch.

The noisy debate has involved audience research firms, network television researchers, advertising agency personnel, and advertisers themselves. At issue is what methods and tools yield the "best" portrait of the viewing audience. The most recent chapter in audience research came in recent months when AGB, a British firm that pioneered the newest recording device, the "people meter," challenged the supremacy of the A.C. Nielsen Co. Nielsen eventually adopted the technology of its British competitor, although the two firms produce an audience sample with somewhat different demographics.

So far, who cares? It seems that the networks do because the representativeness of the sample can be helpful or harmful to their audience. The various audience research firms either under- or over-represent some characteristics of their audience. Advertising agencies and their clients watch warily as one system of audience measurement is being dismantled and replaced by another.

All this occurs amid an upheaval in the communication industry in which audience loyalty is spread out among more and more competitors, from the broadcast networks and local stations to cable and pay cable systems. In this highly competitive world, we have (for better or worse) a television regime that watches rating points with fearsome attention. It is not that everyone is convinced that the present system or the one that will replace it this season represents the best of social science. It does not and most critics acknowledge this, saying that the measurement and monitoring of the American audience is, at best, based on a series of understandings and assumptions between the producers and distributors of television programming and the advertisers who pay for it. What we have, of course, are a series of vested interests: the audience research firms want to sell their services; the

AUTHOR'S NOTE: This essay first appeared in the September 1987 issue of *Communique*, the newsletter of the Gannett Center for Media Studies.

networks want to get the best possible rating; and the ad agencies want their clients to be happy with the result.

In such a system no one really speaks for the public. It is assumed that the public "votes with its eyes" and thus ultimately determines what programming will be aired. But with the ratings themselves in such fragile shape, it is sometimes difficult to determine real "winners and losers" until it is too late.

Leo Bogart, the distinguished communication researcher, has said that audience research is really "an instrument of power." Its problems and imprecisions are well known to those who do the research, Dr. Bogart said, and there seems little impetus for real change.

All parties involved with ratings have, in effect, accepted a system of witch doctors, and the question today is what witch doctor's formula will win out, becoming perhaps a new industry standard.

If we were to begin anew, employing the most modern methods, we could develop a system that is more rigorous and more precise. But as Leo Bogart wisely observed, not many people want that.

Perhaps the current controversy provided the best opportunity in years to sort out the audience-preference dilemma. Whether the broadcasting industry and the advertisers should slavishly accept quantitative measurements as the sole determinant of television programming is another subject for another time, but in the meanwhile someone should be taking the public's role in the current debate.

Some say that is the role of the government in overseeing a regulated industry, but others point out that the industry is less and less regulated. In any case, Congressional hearings on topics of this kind rarely produce creative solutions.

Media scholars, who frequently complain that no one listens to them in the industry corridors where decisions are made, have a singular contribution to make. As independent researchers, they could help find acceptable pathways out of the dilemma. This is not simply a research problem, but a public policy problem that deserves our best efforts and instincts. It is time for people who know what they are talking about, and who care about the public interest, to speak up and join what promises to be a lengthy debate. And it might be said that what goes for television goes as well for other media. Controversies have raged over newspaper and magazine circulation figures and what they mean.

Clearly, people who know and understand audience measurement form quantitative and qualitative perspectives, who represent the industry and the public, need to grapple with some basic issues that determine what we watch on television, listen to on the radio, and read in the print media.

References

Aumente, Jerome. 1987. *New Electronic Pathways: Videotex, Teletext and Online Databases.* Newbury Park, CA: Sage.

Besen, Stanley M., Thomas G. Krattenmaker, Richard A. Metzger, Jr., and John R. Woodbury. 1984. *Misregulating Television: Network Dominance and the FCC.* Chicago: University of Chicago Press.

Boyer, Peter J. 1988. *Who Killed CBS? The Undoing of America's Number One News Network.* New York: Random House.

Cose, Ellis. 1989. *The Press.* New York: William Morrow.

Fox, Stephen. 1984. *Mirror Makers: A History of American Advertising and Its Creators.* New York: William Morrow.

Gannett Center Journal, Vol. 1, No. 1, "The Business of News." New York, Gannett Center for Media Studies, Spring 1987.

Gannett Center Journal, Vol. 2, No. 3, "Measuring the Audience." New York, Gannett Center for Media Studies, Summer 1988.

Ghiglione, Loren. 1984. *Buying and Selling of America's Newspapers.* Indianapolis: R.J. Berg & Company.

Mayer, Martin. 1987. *Making News.* Garden City, NY: Doubleday.

Picard, Robert. 1990. *Media Economics.* Newbury Park: Sage.

Wilson, Clint C., II, and Félix Gutiérrez. 1985. *Minorities and Media: Diversity and the End of Mass Communication.* Beverly Hills: Sage.

Figure 4.1 Reprinted by permission of Clyde Wells, *The Augusta Chronicle.*

4

Covering Politics and Elections

Memo to the Press: Let's Have Fair Play

When public controversy pits the news media against a politician, as it did in January 1988 when Dan Rather and George Bush dueled, if only briefly, the central question is one of fairness: Was Dan Rather fair to George Bush? Was it proper for a news anchor to be a hard-driving, on-the-air reporter in the style of *60 Minutes*? Was the program's abrupt ending fair? Was George Bush's questioning of Rather fair? Was the public well served by the encounter and the report? These questions will be irrelevant with the passing of time, but questions like them will recur in every community in encounters between the media and news sources, whether public officials or others.

The important question here is whether the way we cover and report the news is compatible with fairness, or whether news judgments that ferret out conflict are, by their nature, divergent from fair play. In many instances, I believe, the nature of news and the way it is covered do not always result in fair play and certainly not in any sense of equity. Nor do I believe that they need to.

The recent coinciding anniversaries — those for the bicentennial of the Constitution last year and the sesquicentennial of the telegraph this year —

AUTHOR'S NOTE: Speech given at the Virginia Associated Press newspapers annual meeting, Richmond, Virginia, March 5, 1988; an edited version appeared in the *RTNDA Communicator*, Nov. 1988.

provide us with a legacy and some lessons that are worth noting as we take up this matter of fairness. During the bicentennial celebrations we all prided ourselves on freedom and tried our best to build a consensus of understanding for the meaning of the Constitution. In a speech at the Smithsonian Institution last year, I made a plea to the news media to move from this general concern about our constitutional faith to a quite specific application in 1988. I suggested that we use 1988 to have a self-conscious case study of freedom of the press, not only by offering the best possible coverage, but also by taking our readers and viewers backstage so they can better appreciate the process of the news, how decisions are made, what resources are used, and what conflicts occur. I can think of no better way to demonstrate what freedom of the press is all about than using the coverage of "Election '88" as proof positive that our media do offer something very special indeed, something that is vital to democracy itself. This would move well beyond the house ads and editorials which signaled our general concern last year.

Although the 150th anniversary of the telegraph is not the most riveting anniversary for many Americans, it ought to have some special meaning for AP newspaper editors. And there is a lesson in it. If we had the capability of projecting what the impact of the computer will be on society in the same way we can now look back at the contributions of the telegraph, we would certainly take notice of this anniversary and the profound changes it signaled. James W. Carey and other students of the telegraph point out that it brought us standard time — the United States had a virtually infinite number of time zones prior to 1883 — and it also brought us the futures market. Of course, the telegraph made possible the Associated Press and, more to the point today, it brought us the so-called "telegraph report," wire editors, and much more. It also significantly shaped the standards and style of American journalism. Publishers then and now were frugal people. They didn't want to pay for long, interminable reports in the florid style of the day. So wire reports became clipped, staccato treatments, and for a time newspaper readers could distinguish between the so-called *telegraph stories* and more formal *journalistic* reports.

In time, journalistic styles blended together, and we got the famous AP lead and the inverted pyramid story form as a direct result of the telegraph. We became more efficient and did more structured writing and reporting. And, of course, it was shorter. Surely, the serious journalists of the 1850s must have despaired these developments in the same way that today's critics lament the news nuggets of *USA Today*.

Along with the AP lead came information presented in a descending order of importance and, eventually, a journalistic practice called "objectivity."

Objectivity was never a clinical term universally accepted, but it did illuminate an approach to journalism that stood against bias and in favor of impartiality. It became a proud achievement, a crown jewel in American journalism, as our reporting, unlike that of European papers, moved away from party politics and heavy-breathing ideology to establish a functional difference between news columns and editorial columns.

The upheavals of the 1960s and a reassessment of journalism's role in society, not to mention a journalistic revolution, shelved the concept of objectivity pretty dramatically. In time, editors and others shied away from claims of objectivity which anyone who had ever taken a psychology course knew was utterly impossible, and opted instead for something we came to call fairness. For many, fairness was just a convenient euphemism for objectivity, but to others it represented a more thoughtful articulation of disinterested reporting that covered all the bases rather than simply "balancing" two sides. In sum, it recognized the complexity of news gathering and news decision making and moved away from simplistic formulations which were unsatisfactory both to journalists and their critics.

Thus fairness replaced objectivity and became an article of journalistic faith. If you ask most journalists what one word they would have the public associate with them and their work, I suspect that word would be *fair*. Happily this is a far more noble response than that made by U.S. Senators in a recent study in which they said they preferred to be known as "hardworking."

When thoughtful people are asked to define fairness, they most often beg the question or answer that fairness is accuracy. To be sure, accuracy is a vital element in any notion of fairness, but it does not tell the whole story. When you ask readers and viewers about fairness, they are more likely to return to such notions as *balance, fair play, the level playing field, positive and negative attributes in stories*, and material that is *believable*. Indeed, the well-known Times Mirror study of media credibility actually equates credibility with believability and argues that the media are well regarded by the citizenry, something that other students of public trust dispute.

A recent inventory of the amount of time the national network news shows have devoted to the 13 presidential candidates in 1987 is quite revealing. In a study that recorded 132 minutes devoted to covering Gary Hart and 14 times less to Pete du Pont, the idea of fairness is tested severely.

How well are the media doing their job in covering the 1988 election? It depends, of course, on whom you ask. The public is circumspect, with 80 percent in a recent national poll saying that they feel the coverage of Iowa and New Hampshire is out of proportion. Also on the downside is the finding of 54 percent who say that the media make it harder, not easier, for voters to choose the best person for President. In responding to other questions, citizens in the *USA Today*/CNN poll, also argue that reporters are too aggressive in questioning candidates.

These are public attitudes expressed shortly after the Bush-Rather encounter, but even if slightly more negative than they might be on a slow news day, they paint an unfortunate picture of the state of relations between the public and the media. As a careful observer of what the press is doing this election year, I think these public responses are outrageous and do not reflect the true scope, quality, or quantity of coverage at all. The public, of course, does not have the long view of these matters and reacts somewhat emotionally to news of the moment.

Much of this disparity between what I think is an improving quality of political reporting, which can be documented in many, many ways, and the negative tone of public reaction rests on the doorstep of fairness: the public view versus the press view. The public studies show the public really does not internalize the concept of news very well and does not share the media's notion of fairness either.

Now, recognizing that there are important qualitative factors here that take us well beyond the simple quantification, we know that Gary Hart got more coverage in 1987 for some quite specific reasons: he began the year as the front-runner, was more visible than other candidates, got involved in a scandal, fought with the press, and finally reentered the race. This is the stuff that makes news. None of the other candidates came close to intersecting with news values in such dramatic fashion. Of course in this case we know that Gary Hart himself would have preferred that he had not gotten some of that coverage. Think of it, though. To the public, these figures are outrageous and do not give aid or comfort to the idea that the media are fair. And before you say, "Oh this is television," I can assure you that similar ratios exist in print media coverage for the same period. What happened, of course, was that the principles of newsworthiness were in play. They covered those items that were regarded as most important and most pertinent to the audience, whether in a positive or negative light.

But the results certainly did not meet the layman's test of fairness. To the public, fairness means equal time and equal space, giving all of the candidates about the same treatment. In this election season, it might also mean giving equitable treatment to the various primaries and caucuses, not overplaying Iowa and New Hampshire or giving short shrift to California or New York. It might even mean some kind of balance between positive and negative news. Since most news has a negative tone, many citizen critics argue that they want to see more "good news" that illuminates positive attributes of our public life. Naturally, the coverage of presidential candidates does not meet these standards of fairness. If the press was consistent in applying standards of news judgments and arguing that this was, in fact, its idea of fairness, that would be one thing, but during an election year the media want to play it both ways. They want to exercise traditional news standards, which make no provision for equal treatment, and also attempt to apply some notion of equity to some quite selected coverage areas.

For example, since public attention to the matter of fairness is most acute in an election year, because it is easy to see how individual candidates are treated, the press bends over backwards to promote the idea of fairness. Some specific examples:

When the media cover the national nominating conventions, one convention may be a donnybrook with the party nominee in doubt. The other may be a sort of coronation, wherein the convention is rather pro forma. Now, one is obviously more newsworthy than the other, but you can bet that in print and broadcast media the two will get about the same amount of coverage unless there is some truly deviant aspect of the convention such as the fracas in Chicago in 1968. Even in situations like that, one network television often covers the "other convention" asking why there are not more demonstrations.

Another example: Once the nominating conventions are concluded and there are two candidates, some editors actually measure the amount each candidate gets each day, trying, apparently, to mechanically balance the coverage. Television does the same thing. Here we find the media applying the public standard of equal time and equal space, which they otherwise reject as inconsistent with news values. So it is not surprising that people are confused by these conflicting standards. The public is getting a mixed message.

Thus, I think we need to flesh out fairness, to define it more carefully and in a fashion that not only articulates the case for news judgment as a vital variable, but also tunes into the public's concerns about balance. We need to say forthrightly that *fairness requires accuracy and careful reporting but that accuracy is not enough, for facts and truth are not always one and the same.* Fairness is attempting to be *impartial and professional* in gathering, processing and disseminating the news.

To me fairness means:

1. *Coherent presentation of the facts*, of the basic elements and information required to know and understand the subject being reported.

2. A *context and background* that provides connections to the past and to concurrent issues, events and personalities.

3. *More systematic information-gathering,* making as efficient use as possible of many sources of information and in enough depth to enhance understanding. No critical stone should be left unturned or, if it is, the reader or viewer should be told.

4. *Quality control of information.* The role of the news media is to distinguish the important from the unimportant, reputable sources from unreliable ones. The media should make it clear whether information is being cited or quoted, with approval or not.

5. *More equitable sense-making and interpretation.* There is a profound need for the reporter and editor to be mapmaker, to offer a perspective on the many viewpoints and interests that shape the news and to render those voices with the right intensity and pitch.

Finally, I think we need to reconcile our standards of news and the public's sense of fair play. One way to do that is to create a level playing field in covering the 1988 elections, from the caucuses and primaries through the general election at the local, state, and national level. I think we should let the public go behind the scenes in our newsrooms, either literally or symbolically. This post-bicentennial year provides an unprecedented opportunity to do the kind of high-quality reporting I have spoken of and at the same time to share our manner, methods, and purposes with the people we serve, the readers, and viewers.

How to do this? I think there are several ways. First, we should make a map, give the public a dance card of coverage to come. How are we planning to cover the election? To what extent will we focus on personalities and character, issues, events, candidates' bases of support, the role of special interests, public opinion, and probable public policy outcomes of particular candidate platforms and proposals? People ought to know how the campaigns are being staffed: what is being spent, who is spending it, and what the magnitude of the effort is. How does it compare to the last general election?

Second, we ought to encourage the effort to get inside our collective reportorial heads to get a glimmering of the "rules," whether the conventions and practices of past presidential campaign coverage are changing, and, if so, why.

Third, we need to explain journalistic choices. What is not being covered during an election year? What typical fare is being crowded out? How is it determined that one candidate or one issue deserves considerably more treatment than another?

Fourth, we need to listen to the public and set up regular and routine channels for feedback, whether through focus groups, market research, or community "listening posts." We need to solicit pertinent criticism and be responsive to it when appropriate. And we need to tell the public we are doing this.

If we do these things, I believe we will honor the recently concluded 200th anniversary of our Constitution and the current 150th anniversary of the telegraph in a manner that will make a difference. Thus we could close the gap between the newsworthy and the fair, and strengthen the place of our media in their communities and in the lives of the citizenry.

Election '88 and Voices from the Sky

As the 1988 campaign for the presidency moves through the caucus and primary stage, there is something deeply disturbing about the role of the news media, both print and electronic, in the process.

They seem more contradictory and intrusive in this election than in any before, sending mixed messages to the public they serve and the candidates they portray.

Throughout the summer and during the fall of 1987, the dominant stories about the campaign focused on the character issue and involved George Bush, Gary Hart, Joseph Biden, Michael Dukakis, Pat Robertson, Jesse Jackson, and others. With ferocity, the major media probed the personal lives of the candidates looking for evidence of their fitness for high office.

Still, while the preponderance of coverage of the campaign to date has dealt more with personalities and events rather than issues or matters of probable public policy, I believe that the public is better served in 1988 than ever before in recent times. The reason is not journalistic competence, however, but a new player on the American campaign trail: technology.

Technology is helping media cover the campaign in the most competitive manner possible and, at the same time, is helping candidates take their appeal directly to the voters, by-passing the media. Satellites, cable television, and computers are important new tools in this campaign.

Satellites have brought us nationally distributed newspapers like the *Wall Street Journal*, the *New York Times*, *USA Today* and the *Christian Science Monitor*. Satellites also allow the major networks — ABC, CBS, and NBC — to set up a two-way loop with their affiliate stations and relay information with frightening speed.

On a regional level, broadcasters are doing direct-broadcast hookups, connecting local stations and new networks. Many of these activities did not exist in 1980 when Jimmy Carter and Ronald Reagan squared off. More sophisticated computers permit fast, graphically displayed polling, and have given rise to the Election News Service, a specialized data-base.

Especially notable is cable coverage of the campaign: Ted Turner's Cable News Network, which is doing detailed daily reports in addition to its usual 24-hour feed, and its C-SPAN coverage, which has carried most of the many debates that have been held this year.

AUTHOR'S NOTE: This essay first appeared in the March 1988 issue of *Communique*, the newsletter of the Gannett Center for Media Studies.

Candidates are also benefiting from the new technology. They use video cassettes, mailing them to local campaign committees to be played on VCRs in people's homes, in coffee shops, and meeting houses. They continue to buy advertising in the traditional way, but they can also get their messages around at a modest cost courtesy of satellite transmission, sending up electronic news releases that are sometimes used by local stations or cable systems. All these services are paid for by the candidates.

The question, of course, is whether more information is necessarily better information. There is certainly more coverage: More debates are being beamed to more households than ever before; both broadcast and print coverage of the campaign has been extensive; and even the candidates' basic speeches have been widely disseminated and broadcast as never before, courtesy of the *New York Times,* National Public Radio, and "The Mac-Neil/Lehrer News Hour."

To what extent all this is useful to the voter is yet to be determined. At the moment, the attentive voter who wants to know about any or all of the candidates may choose from a vast array of information sources.

For most voters, though, the coverage of the campaign is, and will likely continue to be confusing. There are too many primaries and caucuses, too many issues and problems to find a simplified solution for real under-standing. And, to top it off, the media have breathed very heavily over this campaign, often changing the traditional rules, acting as chief sermonizer, enforcer of moral values, and arbiter of issues.

To a large extent that role is the result of the declining power of the parties; to a lesser extent it reflects the declining influence of the family, the school, and the church. In any case, it is rarely the result of any conspiracy or even self-conscious awareness among media people.

Of course no one really knows whether, or to what extent, the coverage of a campaign actually affects an election. It used to be said that the media tell us not what to think, but what to think about — which issues and which candidates.

Now I am not so sure that there is not a very concerted effort to influence thinking in a new and quite profound way: not to trumpet the virtues of a given candidate, but, by default, to set the rules of the campaign and to chronicle the events, issues, and people we will truly remember.

Covering the National Political Conventions

As thousands of journalists descend on Atlanta and New Orleans this summer to cover the Democratic and Republican National Conventions, they will greatly outnumber delegates, party operatives, and other functionaries. While purportedly there to "cover the convention," the media will engage less in news coverage than in the conduct of a national pageant.

There was a time when conventions made decisions about candidates and platforms, and no one really knew the outcome until after the roll call. In a strictly literal and legalistic sense the conventions still nominate candidates and promulgate platforms or statement or party principles, but today they usually hold few surprises. Now they are media events wherein the sources of news (e.g., delegates and candidates) are often less important and influential than members of the press corps, especially television anchors, reporters, and commentators, as well as some leading print journalists.

This has been true for some time now, although the media often act as though it were otherwise, injecting hype into a highly predictable, ritualistic process.

Newsweek was prophetic in 1948 when it declared that the conventions of that year "sounded the end of the old-type convention put on for the immediate benefit of the state delegates. Hereafter the show would be played to the camera and microphones and the millions of voters who also watched and listened." In the magazine's view, "Television's first big assignment had won it a permanent byline."

Still, it took some time for party operatives to wake up to this reality.

In 1952, Edward R. Murrow, annoyed that reporters were barred from the convention floor, threatened, "If you throw us out, you're going to have to do it bodily, and I want to remind you that three networks will televise the event." Subsequently there have been other notable scraps between convention officials and reporters, but they have mostly given way to a process that preens itself with publicity.

What the media are covering at the 1988 conventions is a process much less important and newsworthy than it once was.

While the conventions will get enormous coverage and might even be the scene of genuine controversy, they have been visibly brokered in advance by the greatest number of state primaries and caucuses in our history.

AUTHOR'S NOTE: This essay first appeared in the July/August issue of *Communique*, the newsletter of the Gannett Center for Media Studies.

There are few discretionary votes and little chance for last-minute deals to have any real impact. Sessions of Congress and state legislatures are far less predictable than the conventions, which are rapidly becoming politicized versions of Macy's Thanksgiving Day Parade, colorful pageants, and little more.

But convention coverage is not without value. While there is less hard news, there are more challenges to capture the timbre of American life, to identify the values that find their way to the convention and the interests that compete for influence there.

Some commentators, in fact, have suggested that the conventions are well-packaged and colorful civics lessons and that the media do a great national service in covering them. The challenge, of course, is to make that lesson vital and intriguing enough to hold an audience whose attention is easily diverted. The story of American federalism, of regional differences, of our 50 different versions of the same political parties, and of the great issues we so vigorously debate can be compelling.

The media seriously risk their credibility, however, when they posture and pretend, treating inconsequential aspects of the conventions with importance. Convention coverage should not take on the characteristics of sports commentary.

Even the most grizzled news veterans will recognize that the 1988 conventions are visible indicators of great change both in the political process and among the media themselves. These conventions not only play a different role than those of the past, but they will be covered by news media of vastly different capabilities, especially with the technological tools of the computer, communications satellites, and cable.

The most compelling question for the media is what they will do with the new conditions for this convention and the tools available to them to enhance their coverage of it.

Whether television and print can respond to fundamental change in our political process, conveying this important story with context and nuance, may have a lot to do with convention coverage of the future.

There is a chance that conventions will be reduced to the perfunctory coverage now afforded the Electoral College. That would be a loss for the public — and the media.

Politics, Privilege, and the Press

From the time of the penny press, our news media have identified with the "common person" as opposed to those with great wealth, privilege, or power. Slogans like "afflicting the comfortable and comforting the afflicted" are found in the rhetoric of the American revolution and still live in many newsrooms.

And yet we Americans and our news media are really quite ambivalent about privilege. While people in public life, especially those in public office, are supposed to personify an egalitarian ideal, we also preen ourselves on tales of the rich and famous.

When it comes to presidential politics, it is clear that our media coverage lacks any systematic (and some would say fair-minded) approach to matters of deprivation and wealth. When a candidate comes out of poverty, there is a tendency for the press to look for flaws born of deprivation, and the tone of such stories is often more negative than admiring. Both Richard Nixon and Gary Hart got scrutiny of this sort. Coverage of relative wealth, on the other hand, gets more ambivalent treatment. The Kennedys and the Kennedy family, for example, have long been accorded the kind of deference due royalty, even in their worst public moments.

All four of the 1988 presidential and vice-presidential nominees come from somewhat privileged circumstances, a fact the media noted in their reports on the candidates' backgrounds, but only one candidate, Dan Quayle, has been subjected to much scrutiny about his privileged youth and the way he used its advantages. The press does not know quite how to handle this condition, and the reason may be that honest attempts to impose impartial standards on the campaign and the candidate constantly collide with the media's ideological abhorrence of wealth, power, and privilege.

There must be a fragile line where the inappropriate exploitation of privilege violates our sense of fair play. When a call to help a young man get a job or a place in the National Guard deprives others of the same opportunity (or worse, perhaps, disadvantages those less fortunate) then what is otherwise a routine practice becomes suspect in the eyes of reporters. Recall that Dan Quayle was not the first candidate in the 1988 campaign about whom the role of privilege in military assignments was raised. Pat Robertson's military record and questions about his father's influence were raised earlier.

AUTHOR'S NOTE: This essay first appeared in the September 1988 issue of *Communique*, the newsletter of the Gannett Center for Media Studies.

If there is a moral lesson here, it seems to be a not-so-subtle media sermon that privilege is somehow unsavory and must not be exercised indiscreetly.

Ironically, however, there are few institutions where genes, romance, and nepotism play a greater role than they do in the media. By constitutional command our media are quasi-public institutions, but they are often ruled by baronial families and executives for whom special privilege and nepotism are an established way of life. Indeed, Dan Quayle is such a person, the grandson of an influential and politically powerful press baron, Eugene Pulliam.

In this confused controversy, the press is at once fair-minded, giving extraordinary scrutiny to "one of their own," while at the same time being hypocritical by not establishing any sense of when the exercise of privilege is significant enough to challenge a candidate's fitness for public office.

There is not even a clear sense of when privilege is newsworthy, though in the case of Dan Quayle the privilege issue got caught up in patriotism, the Vietnam war, and other emotionally charged subjects.

In the end, the importance of any candidate's background lies in its pertinence to the office he or she is seeking. On matters of corruption and dishonesty, the rules of relentless exposure are clear, but on opportunistic exploitation of one's background, wealth, or influence journalistic folklore and pejorative analysis sometimes cloud news judgment in a way that undoubtedly challenges credibility.

Coverage of the Quayle candidacy and others now fading from memory warrant a full-scale review when this campaign is over. The media in 1988 have done some quite distinguished work, but have also confused the public debate with a wilderness of singular instance often devoid of coherent and comprehensive tracking of candidates, their views, the issues, and their probable impact on life in the public arena.

References

Arterton, F. Christopher. 1984. *Media Politics: The News Strategies of Presidential Campaigns.* Lexington, MA: D.C. Heath.

Barber, James David. 1980. *Pulse of Politics: Electing Presidents in the Media Age.* New York: W.W. Norton.

Bennett, W. Lance. 1983. *News: The Politics of Illusion.* New York: Longman.

Donaldson, Sam. 1987. *Hold On, Mr. President.* New York: Random House.

Gannett Center Journal, Vol. 2, No. 4, "The New Elector." New York, Gannett Center for Media Studies, Fall 1988.

Hess, Stephen. 1981. *Washington Reporters*. Washington, DC: Brookings Institution.
Jamieson, Kathleen Hall. 1984. *Packaging the Presidency: History & Criticism of Presidential Campaign Advertising*. New York: Oxford University Press.
Lang, Gladys Engel, and Kurt Lang. 1984. *Politics and Television Reviewed*. Beverly Hills: Sage.

Figure 5.1
SOURCE: Drawing by Ziegler; © 1983. The New Yorker magazine, Inc.

5

Improving Media Content

Quality Control for the Media

The recent upheaval at CBS was an extraordinary and telling event. Treated with an avalanche of news coverage comparable to that given to the collapse of a government in Western Europe, the events at CBS — and what we have learned through the media about them — may be the first great lesson of the information society. This is an age of communication, and, make no mistake about it, the media industries are important, both as economic players in the marketplace and as newsmakers themselves.

Gone are the days when newspaper editors harrumphed and sneeringly refused to cover television or other newspapers as a story. The axiom that "the snuffbox never sneezes," told to me once by an editor in Minneapolis who did not believe that the media should ever report on themselves, now seems as dated as the hoola hoop.

What happened in the wake of corporate changes at CBS was a seemingly endless stream of news coverage that brought out media pundits and busybodies in droves. It seemed that the press was joining en masse to dissect and protest what had happened to the house built by William Paley (and Frank Stanton) and given its soul by Edward R. Murrow. A good many newspaper and magazine accounts, with little subtlety, seemed to gloat over the network news by Madison Avenue, Wall Street, and Hollywood. In an

AUTHOR'S NOTE: Speech delivered to the Miami International Press Club, Miami, Florida, September 30, 1986, and originally published in *Vital Speeches of the Day*.

orgy of sanctimonious handwringing, we were told that the money managers had entered the temple and were, in effect, undermining news itself. A once great news organization, it was said, had lost its direction and its soul.

What happened at CBS is not a singular instance. Nor did it occur in a vacuum. In fact, the events at CBS are actually quite representative of a much broader problem that exists throughout the news business. It should be seen as a warning both to the public and to all organizations dedicated to gathering and disseminating real news.

In spite of contrary protestations, news *is* a profit center in broadcasting, as it has always been in the print media. Indeed, pious print critics would do well to remember that news as a profit center in television is a relatively recent phenomenon, whereas news has always been the commodity that has driven the economics of newspapers. And newspapers have demonstrated quite convincingly, I believe, that quality journalism can also be commercially successful journalism.

Still, we should look carefully at the turmoil at CBS for lessons that go far beyond the boardroom at Black Rock and into the homes of most Americans. Clearly there is something different in the air. The economic problems of broadcasting today are of almost revolutionary proportions. For the first time in broadcasting's history, advertising revenues have slowed to the point where both CBS and ABC have cut their advertising rates. The shock of that unparalleled circumstance came after the slow realization that the era of continuing inflationary rates and almost limitless demand were about to come to an end. Since news at the networks, once exempt from profit and loss statements, is now viewed as an important profit center, it is inevitable that it should be caught up in the panic to stop the bleeding.

Ever since CBS' highly successful *60 Minutes* became commercially profitable in the 1970s, news divisions were under that inevitable pressure to generate huge profits at a relatively low cost. Television news, once exempted from these pressures, was subjected to all the basic rules of other programming, namely, maximize the audience in order to maximize profits.

Once news executives understood the formula, they understood the results, and change came swiftly. We saw the virtual disappearance of serious documentaries in prime time and the emergence of slick, new journalistic efforts such as *West 57th,* which at times was hard to distinguish from fictional TV efforts (such as the sainted *Miami Vice*) and which some people say was yuppie journalism meeting MTV. In a move that demonstrates the changing priorities, CBS News, the inheritor of the Murrow mantle, hired Phyllis George to anchor a morning news show. This turned out to be a desperate move that only delayed the inevitable: cancellation because of low rating. For some critics, the last straw was the changing nature of the *CBS Evening News.* As long as *CBS Evening News* maintained its rating dominance, inherited from the Cronkite era, things were fine. But as the ratings slipped, CBS News began to lose its grip and its confidence. In this nervous and unsettling atmosphere, debates raged about sweaters, sets, new studios, the color of Dan Rather's hair, and so on, and whether or not he was serious when he signed off "courage." Then it finally spilled over the top. Still, the story came in fragments.

Bill Moyers announced he would quit in November, and then went on the record with many thoughtful observations about the current state of network journalism, while revealing that he had no desire to compete with stories about "three-legged sheep," a piece the CBS Evening News had actually done. *60 Minutes* correspondent Andy Rooney blasted CBS news' policy in his syndicated newspaper column and appeared at the U.S. Open wearing an NBC sports cap! The fever broke during the second week of September, when action by the network's board of directors led to the resignation of both Chairman Tom Wyman and News President Van Gordon Sauter. The press outdid itself the next day. There were lurid headlines and breathy, detailed accounts of the "star-studded" board meeting. As is too often the case these days, it was a Wall Street "observer" who had the last word. What CBS really needed right now, he said, was another Michael Jackson hit. Wall Street said networks must be "clean and mean"—this from grossly fat entrepreneurs who start some Harvard MBAs out at $80,000 a year!

Of course, the problems at CBS were not confined to the news division. Still, the news connection here is an indicator of larger problems that make us wonder whether news values can survive in an increasingly competitive world.

What lessons can we learn from the CBS experience? What is the relevance for the rest of the news business? The CBS episode reminds us of at least two things. One is that news, whether it be television or print, is business, and more than ever is controlled by events that are not necessarily compatible with good journalism, no matter how it is defined. Second, in order for the news business to survive and sustain its credibility, it must rededicate itself to a concept of quality.

A reflective view of the dilemma at CBS and in all of broadcasting (and, indeed, in all media) reveals a feverish competition for the audience in an age of great change. Like other "products," news programs and newspapers are marketed to maximize their audiences. Once seen as "mass media," reaching a large, undifferentiated audience, they now seek out particular readers and viewers and have moved from an economy based on the law of large numbers to a law of right numbers, courtesy of demographics and market segmentation.

Certainly newspapers have not been exempt from this preoccupation with product and markets. Indeed, it is not unusual to hear distinguished editors talk about their papers as products, although not usually as a commodity. The downturn in newspaper circulation a few years ago was dramatically underscored by the death of so many big city dailies, a phenomenon that also brought us the one-newspaper town. This response from the newspaper industry was not unlike that of broadcasters today. They did research and tried to position themselves more effectively to have the competitive advantage with advertisers. The results included special sections, more attractive graphic presentations, brighter writing, and more feature material. Whether this diminished the quality and content of public affairs journalism in America is open to debate, although I think that, in general, it did not.

The point is that new technologies and new media have challenged the old order, have wrought change for broadcasting and print media. There is clearly a crisis for news in America; but a crisis is not a catastrophe. It is a time of great change when the warning signals are clearly out.

However craven it may sound, news is and will continue to be a profit center. To me, that only means that it must deliver information of value that the audience wants and needs. In the end, news must be compatible with advertiser support. There will, of course, be competition, and networks may even take on new functions as they compete with satellite entrepreneurs and regional television operations. What this means to me is that the numbers of media outlets in the country may change or may assume new roles in the media family. Like magazines, which have long had birth, maturation and death cycles, our heretofore relatively stable broadcast and newspaper organizations may change markedly and massively. The news magazine may be an endangered species, which is one example of the wrenching changes that are coming. There is nothing magical about the numbers of networks that we have in this country; nothing, I might add, in the Constitution about the big three having inalienable rights. The number of newspapers has similarly had a massive downturn since the turn of the century and has now leveled off. And, indeed, new news organizations and new formats not yet on the drawing board (or electronic screen) may be in the offing.

In the midst of this great change, I believe there are some fundamental values that signal quality in journalism, and in news. I believe further that

journalism is a public trust that, while a business, is more than a business —
one might say, a business with "value added." It does have a constitutional
franchise, one that carries some very special implications.

There are clearly times when great journalism is not necessarily popular
journalism, when a courageous media runs against the tide of mean-spirited
public opinion to take up a just cause. Most of the time, though, people want
and support good journalism, which means information of high quality, well
written and well presented. Every recent study of credibility shows that the
public wants information that has integrity and that helps people navigate in
a world of ever-increasing complexity. So it can be argued that quality
journalism has great value to the media and to the public. It produces useful
and complete information and, thus, fulfills the press's constitutional mandate; and it is also likely to be commercially successful, providing there is
good and competent management. I should add that it is clearly possible to
make large amounts of money by pandering to the lowest possible taste, but,
increasingly, there are highly profitable enterprises that are also centers of
real quality and superb news coverage.

Quality control for journalism is unlikely to occur unless there is a
commitment to high standards of news gathering, editing, and dissemina-
tion at the very top of an organization. Gifted leaders in our communication
industries care about quality; they have a concept that their managers carry
out. There are many organizational factors that can ensure and enhance
quality, but none more important than commitment to people. It is in this
area where I believe the communication industry, especially newspapers
and broadcast stations, are seriously remiss. The failure of many media
organizations to invest in their own people both diminishes the quality of
journalism in America and, in the long run, is also very costly for these
cost-conscious organizations.

What I am talking about are the relatively low salaries in American
journalism, a paucity of opportunity for professional development and mid-
career advancement, the niggardly support for journalism education, and the
failure to actively invest in the best and brightest young Americans who
want to have careers in newspapers and television.

Journalism salaries, while improving all the time and quite good in many
major organizations, are still low in comparison to those paid in other
professions and occupations that demand high-quality, creative work from
people. One of the main results of this is an alarmingly high dropout rate as
people leave the news business for other endeavors. Their leaving is quite
costly for the organizations that have employed them, and I might say, quite

stupid from a management perspective. But beyond salaries, I believe there are a number of things that the press (both print and broadcasting) could do to enhance quality by investing in people.

First, they could develop imaginative in-house training programs, support industry-wide training efforts, and help develop new education and training activities where needed, sometimes in specialized areas of only local or parochial concern. This has worked for other enterprises and has arrested worker dropout.

Second, they should and can support journalism education. Journalism education, not incidentally, has a doubly daunting problem. It faces rejection on the campus from the rest of the university and similar rejection from some in the professional community. As a loving critic of journalism education, I despair at the low quality of some journalism school programs, while feeling pride for others that are truly quality efforts. In the main, though, journalism education needs help, not carping criticism, if it is to truly serve the needs of society and the press. There is no other field I know of where so many top leaders want to devour their own rather than elevate those schools that really are dedicated to improving the field. Some especially committed media professionals deserve a salute for their support of journalism education.

Third, I think it is important that the industry begin to seek out the best and brightest students, from whatever field, urging them to plight their troth with journalism. The record is quite spotty. Newspaper and television executives are incredibly arrogant about their hiring practices. Many of them, at the highest levels, say that all young people must pay their dues before they can be admitted to the quality centers of American journalism.

This is truly one of the media's self-inflicted wounds. Imagine the prospects of the most brilliant graduate of a high quality journalism graduate school versus the prospects of the best and brightest in a law school. Law students are courted by the great firms, not because they have adequate experience or any great immediate value, but because they represent the future. The young person, whether a journalism major or not, who has a profound and demonstrated interest in the media, rarely finds such suitors. Instead, he or she is told to go to a small market and work up. In general, of course, that is good advice. But there should be and, I think, must be a few places guaranteed at the nation's largest and most important newspapers and television stations for young people considering careers in the media but opting for other fields that are more caring, more humane, and more concerned about them as people and as professionals.

Fourth, it seems to me that along with erudition and training goes research. There is a paucity of genuine research and development activity involving people in the news media. This can be done either in-house, by supporting industry and university research organizations; or by commissioning private firms to monitor editorial quality, internal management, audience patterns, and opportunities for news people. This is what other successful enterprises do, and there is no reason why the communication industry should not also become part of the modern world in this regard.

Finally, these activities and others that could be suggested will cost money. They should. Therefore, I believe that all news organizations should dedicate a portion of pre-tax profits to education, training and research development. This will affect people who work in journalism in the short run and will have enormous advantages for the public in the long run. I think it will be good business and will also be good for freedom of expression in America. It can and will likely make journalism more credible.

The great lesson from the CBS affair should not elicit a handwringing lament, but instead a commitment to quality and a quest for better journalism. The current economic upheaval need not undermine the news, but can strengthen it enormously.

The Future of Public Affairs Reporting

Public affairs reporting is the most important mission for American journalism and, perhaps, the principal reason that the press is guaranteed certain rights under the Constitution of the United States. Remember, the Framers were mostly concerned about the free flow of information on public affairs and occurrences.

It may seem curious in this technological age to devote so much time to the future of public affairs reporting in newspapers, which are the most anachronistic and most venerable of media. It was more than 20 years ago that Marshall McLuhan predicted the death of print. Even today we have heard a warning from such commentators as Stuart Loorey of CNN, who says the electronic media has already won the public affairs news battle "hands down." So why bother to devote time to newspapers and public affairs reporting? There are several good reasons. To begin with, the newspaper is still the principal purveyor of public affairs information. It is at the substantive center of the media because of its detailed, comprehensive news coverage. No other medium can make this claim. And, I believe it was this protection of public affairs information that caused the Framers to grant a special place to the press in our constitutional scheme. Those who are involved with entertainment and advertising argue that they, too, have freedom of expression and they doubt it is news and information that have a preeminent place in our system of freedom of expression. The news media, particularly the newspaper and to some extent news magazines, also set the agenda for public affairs reporting for the electronic media which, of course, have the largest audience and reach the most people. Because of its preeminent role as comprehensive news-gatherer and agenda-setter, there is a great case to be made for the newspaper, regardless of the manner in which it might be delivered in the future. Indeed, it might not be on paper at all, but instead transmitted by electronic impulses.

We are reminded by John Wicklein in his book *Electronic Nightmare* that all communication in this country is coming together into a "single electronically-based computer-driven form." Thus, *process is our most important product* (with apologies to General Electric), but I will argue that we should not confuse the *process* of public affairs reporting with the *delivery scheme* it might employ.

AUTHOR'S NOTE: Speech given at the Symposium on Public Affairs Reporting in the Year 2004, Kiplinger Program for Public Affairs Reporting, Ohio State University, Columbus, Ohio, October 1984.

This is a time when public affairs reporting is under siege in many ways. It is under scrutiny, partly because of technology. No one really know how the public affairs report might be altered by such new information services as videotex and teletext and all of the others that could change the nature of the audience and thus the message delivered. We are under a strain today because of the economic factors that face mass communication in America. Sociologists are fond of saying that *the structure is the message, what you do is what you are.* We have moved in this country from a world of small independently owned newspapers to mass media mostly owned and controlled by groups, conglomerates and other enterprises that are no longer locally owned or managed. For many people this is a great concern. Another trend is the apparent nationalization of media with publications like *USA Today,* the *Wall Street Journal,* and national editions of the *New York Times* and the new *Washington Post Weekly,* as well as other publications that change the dimension and scope of public affairs reporting. For these reasons and others, we ask whether superficiality will drive substance out of public affairs reporting and whether entertainment values will overtake the information functions of mass media. These are among the swirling forces we will have to master in order to understand the future of the media and the kind of information they will deliver. Once this is in focus, we can also address the issue of credibility of mass communication.

Does the American public know and understand what mass communication is all about? Do people support the First Amendment? Do they believe what they read and see in the news media? What the polls tell us about public trust in the media is not very encouraging. At the same time there is what Stuart Loorey mentioned: the "First Amendment under siege" with a strain between the government, the media, and the public. Some of this began with court decisions, decisions that were not always covered and interpreted by the press in the most thoughtful fashion. The newspapers cheered some seemingly pro-press decisions in the 1960s, only to rue their existence in the 1980s. All too often a self-serving press has pushed its First Amendment rights with little concern for citizen rights to information or privacy. More than 15 years ago, the legal scholar Alexander Bickel warned us that "the more we define freedom, the less freedom we have." There was something simple, elegant, and wonderful about the command of the First Amendment ("that Congress shall make no law . . . ") before it became so encumbered with court decisions expanding the definition of press rights and duties, and which sometimes assert that the press is "the necessary representative" of the people. With expanded rights come new duties, some of them heretofore unknown and unwelcome. Decisions like these led to the government's case against the *Wall Street Journal*, raising questions as to whether or not the press has a fiduciary responsibility to the public. These are some of the issues we ought to address in any examination of public affairs reporting. We must, of course, try to understand that public affairs reporting is really the principal source of information about government and public policy given the American people.

As we look to the future, we do so with the backdrop of a rich history of public affairs reporting. And, although change is incremental, it does come and it does have meaning. There have been major changes in the styles and standards of American journalism, so we should not be overwhelmed by those so evident today. In 1883, when Manton Marble sold the New York *World* to Joseph Pulitzer, there was great fear that news and comment about public affairs would be diminished by what we would now call the "packaging and marketing" approach Pulitzer represented, and which led to a mass press. Before long, Americans noticed that the president of Harvard no longer wrote long pieces for the front page of the *World* and that the great scientists of the day no longer had access to news columns for unedited essays. Then as now, economic factors brought change.

Sociologists tell us that the structure is the message and a recent journal article says that this means the old slogan "all the news that's fit to print" has been driven out by "news that maximizes profit only." The sociologists tell us that we have entered an era when devotion to the coverage of the institutions that affect our lives (including business and economics) has diminished. And we are told also that group ownership leads to less coverage of conflict and more consensus reporting in local communities. Indeed, there is such research evidence, although not powerful evidence, because it comes from narrow studies in particular communities. What has been written does suggest that there is less diversity in editorial commentary and less coverage of conflict. The whole question of whether group versus individual ownership affects reporting has not been studied thoroughly or well. This topic needs careful, competent examination. Such study will not turn back the clock, but serious findings will be instructive to local editors and staffs seeking improvement. We have examples in this country where group ownership has advanced and elevated local newspapers and we can find instances where superb news-oriented papers were neglected or savaged by the practices of group ownership. This depends on the values and standards that operate within individual corporations. I think that the real fear here is not so much with contemporary media conglomerates, most of whom have an editorial orientation, but with possible future owners such as insurance companies, Arab oil states, or other non-media firms that might attempt to control and manage the news.

The shape of public affairs reporting is, of course, related to economic matters. For example, there has been the rise of the "usepaper." Public affairs reporting has survived in an atmosphere in the last 10 or 12 or 15 years or so when changes occurred as a result of newspapers' response to sagging circulations. As you all know, there were great fears at the dawn of the 1970s that young people in America did not read newspapers and were not very attentive to public affairs news.

As a result there were a number of national initiatives, some of them involving the American Newspaper Publishers Association in cooperation with editors and others, in readership projects that brought market research to bear on questions about the audience. With the help of this research, editors began to align what people said they thought they wanted with what the press could deliver. This led to special sections and the so-called "usepaper." Some criticize *USA Today* as the ultimate usepaper because it gives people what they say they want, all courtesy of readership research.

I would argue a desire to court and serve the audience has always been the case with successful American media and that the history of journalism chronicles the death of many publications that did not pay attention to their audiences. In both broadcasting and print, news consultants told us a good deal about local communities and suggested a realignment first by repackaging the product. This was particularly dramatic for newspapers and brought the emergence of special sections. "Real estate" gave way to "shelter" sections, "society" made way for "life-style," and sports was expanded. Along came "money" sections that brought more coverage of business. Did this packaging push public affairs reporting out of the newspapers? No, it clearly did not! What did happen was a structural evolution that began with repackaging and new graphics. Secondly came the slow but steady reorganization of newsrooms, some of which was tied to technology. Third came changes in the actual presentation of news, both in the writing styles and formats for delivering information. This was, in fact, not bad at all, but very good for public affairs reporting because it made reporting audience-oriented.

What we had heretofore honored and praised in public affairs reporting was a journalism that all too often appealed to the sources of information. The legal reporters of the country were most pleased when leading lawyers and jurists read their work. They sometimes seemed to care less about the rest of the audience. I have gone to meetings of science writers and medical writers, where the reporters actually look like scientists and physicians, and again, they identify more with their sources than their readers and viewers. So this market thrust, I think, is not really a bad thing.

While some editors talked about "soft and sexy in the afternoon," others worried soft news would drive out hard news. What has followed is quite fascinating. There has been a redefinition of news where old-time sports editors look with despair and say, "My God, look what they have done to my sports page." And what have they done? They have started covering new topics like the economics of sports, health and medicine, homosexuality in the locker room, and drug use by athletes. These mainstream public affairs issues are now treated in sports sections of newspapers in a more vigorous manner than in the past. News of housing and apartment seeking and finding (which is dear to my heart at the moment, having moved to New York City in the midst of the greatest housing shortage since the end of World War II) is seen as important public affairs news because it is information that people need. It is more than news of real estate for narrow and self-serving audiences.

Let us turn for a moment to the issues of technological change. The question has come up here this morning and is raised frequently about what new technology might do to public affairs reporting. In Columbus, Ohio where QUBE, an interactive TV system was pioneered, people are acutely aware of the sometimes dashed expectations and deferred dreams associated with technology. Too often we lose our way when we deal with technology because we want instant gratification. We are an instant gratification society where the "chi chi" and "fru fru" is something that we all want.

Because we are the kind of people who want to eat rich foods and still be thin, we are inclined to think if technology does not pay off instantly we should discard it and say, "Well, it probably isn't going to work." For example, what if someone came to you and said there is a possibility of an information system that would tie you into every possible institution in the community with nearly instant access to many individuals, too. And if I added that this new fantastic information service is having some indexing problems at the moment, and is likely to be expensive at first, you might say, "Ah ha, videotex is not going to work; it is a medium whose time has not come." But I am not talking about videotex, I am quoting what people said about the telephone in 1910, 1920, and 1940 when it was still a very expensive medium. Think of the genius of the Yellow Pages and what a complex retrieval system that must have seemed when first introduced. The main uses of the telephone today are to make phone calls to get information about other numbers. It took 100 years in America for the newspaper to reach 50 percent of the population. It took 70 years for the telephone to reach 50 percent of the population, and yet today both the newspaper and the telephone are rituals of daily life.

When we ask whether anyone will really subscribe to an information service that they might not use very often, we should remember that most people subscribe to telephone services that they use very little each day. The phone is an essential element of our daily life, and when we move, we have it installed immediately even though our use for it may be quite limited. Radio and television took only 10 years to reach 50 percent of the American public; cable television, for a variety of reasons mainly dealing, I think, with governmental regulation and economics, took 35 years to reach about 40 percent of the American public. It will probably take another five years to reach more than 50 percent. I do not think we should assume that new information services will not work or that they will not challenge the traditional public affairs report. Perhaps their time has just not come.

In a variety of ways, public affairs reporting could be altered by people's use of the personal computer, which can link us to all kinds of information, such as weather, sports scores, stock quotations, lists, and other information of public record. The American newspaper no doubt will change as more public record information is delivered electronically. It will become the great sense-maker of society and less the purveyor of highly specific information.

Let me return for a moment to the legal-political climate and public attitudes that constitute another swirling social force. It goes by many names: public trust, confidence and credibility. We worry that the public does not know and understand the news media and that given its druthers the public might vote out the First Amendment and the rest of the Bill of Rights. Indeed, polls say as much. I think we have a diagnosis that needs a solution. Although many of the negative assessments about public attitudes toward the media are probably right, there are several overt and subtle reasons why such negative views prevail. One is public ignorance, partly fostered by the press's unwillingness to write about itself. Once when I was doing media criticism, the editor of the *Minneapolis Tribune* responded to one of my columns by first apologizing to his readers, with the comment, "The snuff box never sneezes," saying how inappropriate it was for the press to discuss itself. This is changing because even the press recognizes that it is a major institution in American society. And major institutions warrant continuous scrutiny. Another barrier to public understanding of the media is that American education is incredibly deficient in the area of the media.

This does a great disservice by fostering misunderstanding about the nature and role of mass communication in American society, as well as freedom of expression. We cannot expect the American people to appreciate and understand the media when nobody makes an effort to provide full information. If the Reporters Committee on Freedom of the Press and other friends of the press got less agitated about the courts and more concerned about what the schools do not teach about the media, it might do even more than it does presently to foster press freedom.

Negative public attitudes toward the press are most often associated with a chilling effect on free expression and investigative reports. As you know, there is an increase in libel litigation, and megabuck judgments haunt the press. Much of what we know and don't know about all this is directly related to public affairs reporting and its treatment of law and courts. Many journalists fell in love with the Warren Court and assumed that the tenor and tone of its decisions would go on forever. What constitutional scholars even then recognized as a great judicial revolution was not likely to continue in an upward spiral. Now, there is a tendency to be disappointed with the Burger court and especially its press decisions. Some journalists have suggested the present Supreme Court is a right-wing cabal that is destroying freedom of expression in America. Any constitutional scholar will tell you this is patent nonsense, and still this view is promoted pervasively by the news media in their own self-interest. This is wrong-headed reporting.

Those who cover courts with less emotionalism and more context come to quite different conclusions. Witness the British journal *The Economist* on the tenth anniversary of the Burger court when that magazine declared that the Burger Court was a moderately-liberal court of mostly mediocre men. This is a distant cry from the emotional portrayal of the court seen in much of our media. It is a very different diagnosis than we find in Bob Woodward and Scott Armstrong's book, *The Brethren*, for example. Still, a continuous debate between press and government is healthy. It has gone on since the 1780s and is no more acute today than it was in the past. We must be vigilant, of course, because our press freedom is only as strong as the most recent court decisions, and if we are to have freedom of the press, we must fight for it constantly. This will be a continuous battle because the press is not the only institution in society with rights. Thus, the future of public affairs reporting must be seen against the backdrop of the economic realities we discussed earlier, of technological change and of the socio-political climate, most often seen first in public attitudes and later in court decisions.

We return to an earlier question. Does soft news drive out hard news? Do the new sections, the new graphics and faster information and more humanistic coverage somehow denigrate public affairs reporting? No, I do not think so. Public affairs reporting is stronger than ever before. This was not always the case. As a teacher at the University of Minnesota I coauthored a text on public affairs reporting, not because I had any passion for such a task, but because the three most widely used books at that time were all out of print! And why did these books on public affairs reporting go out of print? Because no publisher thought the market was worth courting.

What has happened to the public affairs report in the midst of change? There is more context today as we see coverage of national trends. We are also witnessing better efforts to connect fragments of news into patterns of continuity. This is the opposite of what Lord Tennyson described when warned about "fragments of singular instance." Public affairs reporting in newspapers and in broadcasting is more conscious of time and of protracted governmental decisions. It now traces the long evolutionary flow in the decisions of government that do not often lend themselves to immediacy and the quick news fix, but need continuity and follow-up. There is also an excellent translation of bureaucratic language in a way that did not happen when, for example, economic reporting was equated with one ignorant reporter interviewing an economist about changing interest rates. The bad old days of reporting resulted in long turgid paragraphs tracing the economist's words in near-stenographic fashion. This kind of reporting is nearly extinct. Now, we see corporate strategy stories and a whole new dimension of business journalism tied closely to public affairs journalism. Now there are stories that tell us what the rules of government are and how policies relate to them. This is absolutely critical in understanding courts and law and legislative bodies. These are positive signs. The newspaper of the future is in good hands if trends like these are harbingers.

What will the newspaper of the future look like? Experts tell us that the newspaper of the future may not be on paper at all, but will continue to be an information enterprise. It will be an information service delivered to us by whatever technology is most economically feasible at the time, and that may indeed be a paper. It will be a smaller paper than the one we see now and it may be produced and transmitted differently. It will be an easily-accessible information medium, not something that you plow through jumping from page to page looking for stories and ferreting out details. If it is successful it will have an indexing system where people can find information quickly and efficiently. It will be comfortable for people — what computer manufacturers call "user friendly."

The newspaper of the future will listen to and learn from its audience. In the same way people at shopping centers often avoid the obscure boutique, going instead to Woolworth's, I think the "paper" must touch people's hearts and their interests. It will tell us about our neighborhoods and our neighbors. It will help us understand what we do and why we do it, even watching television. The newspapers of the future will be information-laden, with wide-ranging information available efficiently and easily.

Finally, it will be a very good advertising vehicle or it will not survive. Economically it will be a precision instrument, not a shotgun. It will operate not by the law of large numbers (which was the way newspapers started as a mass medium), but by the law of right numbers. It will do so by an appeal to a segmented audience and will be part of the world of market segmentation. It will not attempt to appeal to the entire community if it is going to be a serious medium in an America that defends and supports the First Amendment. It must cover the entire community for its audience, but it will learn to distinguish between audience and community, knowing that they are not one and the same. Finally, it is going to have to be cheap. People are not willing to pay substantively for this, although they are willing to pay more than they do now. This is what experts are telling us about the newspaper of the future. I am optimistic about the future of public affairs reporting and do not see the modern trends I have discussed as spelling doom for the public affairs report or as the end of serious investigative reporting. Instead, I see a more compassionate kind of journalism coming as a result of all of these forces.

The Ethics of the News-Business Connection

Professional journalists have always lived in a somewhat schizophrenic world where pious pronouncements about the pursuit of truth coexist with the obvious need of the press to make profits.

The conflict this brings has been intensified in recent years by two parallel, yet seemingly contradictory, trends. One is an accelerated interest in journalistic ethics. The other is an unabashedly commercial "marketing approach to news" that brings the values of the business and editorial operations of newspapers and broadcasting more into harmony.

The question arises as to whether the flurry of interest in ethics is platitudinous ritual or an attempt to make the press more accountable. At the same time thoughtful critics wonder whether the marketing approach to news really militates against ethical practices.

These issues emerge most often when media consultants encourage their clients to inject elements of entertainment into the news. Television news directors are told that they will have a larger and more attentive audience if they use a livelier "happy talk" format. Newspaper editors hear similar promises. They too can fight terminal dullness and expand the audience if they undergo design "face lifts" and make their papers look like sanitized versions of the *New York Post*.

A recent *Wall Street Journal* article focused on the work of newspaper consultant Stuart H. Schwartz, a journalism professor, and his advice to a small Iowa newspaper. Schwartz told the paper's staff to pay heed to market surveys and calibrate both selection and presentation of the news more carefully to the audience preferences. The goal of such media marketing is holding onto the existing audience or expanding it, as well as more carefully commanding only that portion of the audience that is most attractive to advertisers.

Not surprisingly the "news doctors," whether working for print or broadcast media, catch some flak. For Schwartz, exposure in the *Wall Street Journal* brought a flurry of blistering letters and phone calls, one of which said:

"It's people like you who are destroying newspapers in this country . . . you're turning out trash for the sake of money . . . you obviously have no sense of journalism ethics."

AUTHOR'S NOTE: Speech originally delivered before the Minnesota Newspaper Association in 1984 and reprinted in M. Emery and T. Smythe, *Readings in Mass Communication*, W. C. Brown: 1985.

Figure 5.2 Gene Bassett — Atlanta Journal/United Features Syndicate. Reprinted by permission of UFS, Inc.

In a spirited counterattack in *Editor and Publisher,* Schwartz suggested that journalistic ethics had become an excuse for mediocrity. He wrote:

> 'Professional' journalism has become a shield behind which journalists crouch, avoiding responsibility for newspapers that are largely irrelevant to modern life.
>
> Journalists are capable of producing marketable and popular products, but this requires an entirely new approach to (the) daily (news) paper, and a considerable break with the immediate past. It involves the elimination of journalistic traditions that are based upon the notion of an educated elite — newspaper journalists — 'passing down' information to a less privileged populace.
>
> It is time to do away with intellectualizing that does little except widen the gulf between reader and newspaper. Is it possible to be both responsible and popular? Of course — one merely has to change the definition of responsible journalism.
>
> It is time to take newspapers to the people, whose concerns are being ignored by most newspapers. And it is time to cast aside the strange assumption that responsibility demands unpopular newspapers speaking to fewer people; if that's the case, then the ultimate in journalistic responsibility would be going out of business.

Some critics might question whether there is really a conflict between ethics and addressing audience interests. Hasn't the news already been selected and presented in a way as to be most compelling to the reader, listener, or viewer? After all, only papers that are purchased and presumably read can survive. Further, there is a long row of journalistic tombstones stretching back to colonial days marking the graves of publications that lost touch or favor with their readers.

While all this is true, there is something noticeably different today. It is the nature and the intensity of modern efforts to market the newspaper as a product or commodity for sale.

While broadcast news has long been tied to audience ratings, newspapers were slow to buy into modern marketing techniques and procedures. But when they did, they did it with gusto, picking up terms like "product differentiation," "targeting" and others to describe their efforts to reach the audience.

This was, in part, brought about by the decline of newspaper circulation in the late 1960s and early 1970s that led to a national readership project. In the project, paid for by publishers, researchers gathered intelligence about the newspaper reader (and nonreader) and made subsequent recommendations to the nation's print press.

One result of the intensive look at newspaper readership was recommendations for papers to develop special sections, sometimes called "Life-Style," "Weekend," "Shelter" and others all targeted to special segments of the audience. Along with this came a push to reach young readers who had all but forsaken the newspaper reading habit.

With special sections came innovations in old writing styles. Some papers even reorganized their staffs to accommodate the new information patterns and presentation styles ushered in by the marketing of special sections. Often, faltering afternoon papers with acute circulation problems were in the vanguard of what was called the "use paper" movement. Use papers were designed to help the reader **use** the community more effectively. This altered the traditional definition of news and of media content generally.

Some papers were accused of pandering to the lowest tastes; others were chided for becoming more elitist. Newspapers were locked in a feverish battle with broadcasting and other media outlets for the ever-so-fickle reader or viewer, who was now called a "media user."

Consultants told newspaper publishers that they needed to "position" themselves more effectively in order to survive. It was abundantly clear that the size of the audience was not necessarily as important as its composition.

A classic example of this problem was the financially troubled *New York Daily News*, the nation's second largest daily. A lot of people obviously buy the *News*, but not the *right* people.

What is wrong with the trend toward calibration of newspaper package and content to audience interests is, of course, that it runs counter to the professed purpose of the newspaper press which is to cover the community and contribute to the free flow of information.

As a mass medium the newspaper has claimed a special place among the media as the principal beneficiary of the free press clause of the First Amendment. Still, there is no constitutional mandate that the press reach all of the people or even represent their interests.

The newspaper clearly has become part of the total communications mix, rather than a unique medium serving an undifferentiated general audience. What isn't clear now (or in the future) is how and whether *journalism* will distinguish itself from *information*. As information systems with factual and descriptive data become available to a wider segment of the population, will journalism (the selected, ordered and orchestrated information, opinion and entertainment) have any particular appeal?

Perhaps there has always been some marketing mentality among editors, but not until recently did they pay much attention to studies by circulation managers or use marketing and business terms to describe the editorial "product" and editorial decisions. Some editors in an ostrich-like reach for the past say this isn't happening, but clearly at most American dailies marketing decisions dictate the amount of space given the news and other editorial material. They also have a role in determining how the news is to be presented to the reader.

Even as editors give more attention to computer printouts or readership preferences, there is also a non-quantitative humanistic movement among thoughtful journalists who want to improve press performance and make the media more accountable to the public.

Every 30 years or so there is a spate of books on press ethics, but this predictable happening rarely sustains itself for long. However, since the early 1970s, there has been an outpouring of books and articles about press ethics. There have also been many midcareer seminars, conferences, and meetings.

The Ford Foundation even sponsored a roadshow featuring two Harvard law professors who conducted ethics clinics in many cities and states. Universities initiated mediated ethics courses and the subject even got considerable attention in the popular press.

In 1981, the "Year of Janet Cooke," concern about press responsibility and professionalism reached fever pitch. The concern and public comment continues, especially in recent days with revelations about media hoaxes.

The national society of press ombudsmen has been formed and the National News Council was in operation for 10 hears before being disbanded. Although Minnesota is alone among the states with a sustained press council experiment, several other proposals for press accountability have been heard elsewhere.

Media organizations are dusting off and upgrading their codes of ethics. Papers like the *Seattle Times* and *Minneapolis Star and Tribune* have adopted sweeping new codes with specific prohibitions and tough enforcement provisions. Concern over media ethics usually centers on a standard of conduct for journalists and journalistic organizations. Terms like virtue, responsibility, accuracy and truth are typically mentioned.

Such noble, high-minded notions lead to questions about the essential purposes of journalism. For the language of media codes suggests that the press is a great social agency, rather than a profit-making business. One only need look at the code of the American Society of Newspaper Editors, which says journalism's purpose is serving "the welfare of the people," or the Associated Press Managing Editor's devotion to "the truth."

The National Conference of Editorial Writers (always a bit verbose) says it wants to "promote information and guidance toward sound judgments which are essential to the health of democracy." Even the most sentimental social worker would be proud of the Radio and Television News Directors' desire "to promote human respect for the dignity, privacy and well-being of persons with whom the news deals."

The new emphasis on ethics is probably due to the growing realization of the power of the press, especially during the "Communications Presidency" and with much new evidence about the impact and influence of television on people's thinking. This coupled with a general social concern about the responsiveness of social institutions (of which the press is one) gives added momentum to media ethics as a worthy professional pursuit.

People who see a clear conflict between an ethically sensitive press and one that is marketed to meet the expressed desires of its readers often overlook another reality. That is the growing elitism of media personnel and their distance from average citizens.

This is happening not by a conscious desire of reporters and editors to separate themselves or stand apart from (or above) their readers, but because of the changing nature of the journalistic craft or profession.

Studies of media people show that reporters, in particular, are better educated, better paid, and in many ways clearly unlike the rest of the community. They are more liberal politically, less religious, less likely to be married or live in a single-family dwelling. And, less often do reporters frequent the gathering places where other citizens spend their time, namely, laundromats, bowling alleys, and corner taverns. They often have little personal experience in the dominant work places (factories or computer plants) where other people earn their livings. Certainly they are less family oriented.

The improved status of reporters and reporting is a mixed blessing. It is good for the press to have higher quality personnel than in the past, but this also increases the likelihood that the press will be dangerously out-of-touch with its community.

Happily, the marketing approach to news provides media people with important data about their audience and how it differs from the community-at-large. Who subscribes and who doesn't?

At a recent newspaper research conference, for example, a group of editors were shown videotape records of focus-group interviews with *Los Angeles Times* "circulation stops," that is former subscribers who canceled their subscriptions.

This and other information available through modern marketing methods can give editors and reporters much more precise feedback to help in developing a "product" that is both in touch with the readers and produced with high journalistic standards.

There are other important ways that the press can demonstrate that marketing and ethics are not in conflict. One is more open coverage of the media as businesses. Instead of sounding like a sanctimonious politician, the press should 'fess up to what it is — a business with a special public responsibility. This would do much to restore and enhance credibility.

Only a few American newspapers report on themselves in any clear and understandable way. The apparent prohibition in writing about internal power plays, the economic health of the paper and other issues deprives the public of essential information. Of course most citizens know that the press is a business, but they are given much less information about its operation than they can get about other commercial enterprises.

A few papers that have allowed their reporters to pursue their own corporate boardrooms with the same vigor they usually devote to other business news do considerable community service in the process.

Secondly, the media continues to be among the least accountable American businesses or social institutions. A Public Agenda Foundation study in 1981 revealed that this is not lost on the public, which when asked about constraints on freedom of expression did not list the Reagan Administration or Burger Court, but instead pointed the finger at the media, saying, "the press by being closed and inaccessible to most citizens actually works against the individual freedom."

Methods for press accountability may differ from community to community. A press council may work in one place and not in another. The various instruments of press accountability can all help: corrections policies, bureaus of accuracy and fair play, open forum, radio call-in shows featuring editors and broadcasters talking about their own enterprises and other activities. They can be carried out in a professional manner and in a fashion that does not inhibit First Amendment freedom.

The need for a compact based on openness and mutual respect is needed more today than ever before. Journalism must make a case for itself to explain why thoughtful and orderly information presented with interpretive tools and in literate language is more beneficial than raw data ordered up through an information storage and retrieval system.

If journalism does not give persuasive and compelling reasons, it may become obsolete in the coming "every person an editor" era when we can dial-up information without benefit of trained reporters who select and interpret to help make sense of things. Ethical journalists devoted to marketing the best possible product can do much to enhance freedom of expression in America.

On Investigative Reporting

On my way to the 1986 Investigative Reporters and Editors convention in Portland, I met an editor friend who expressed some surprise at my destination. "The IRE," he said, "how very 1970s. I didn't realize those people were still around. They must be fossils by now."

The idea that investigative reporting is "very 1970s" is somewhat unsettling. It's a common idea, I think, and one that accurately reflects the diminished interest in investigative reporting today, both in the newsrooms and on the campuses. Indeed, a number of the nation's finest investigative reporters have lost their jobs; even as they are accepting accolades for their work, they are also looking for someone to hire them. Indeed, several investigative units have either shut down or pursue fewer stories at a time when the climate for investigative work seems quite fragile.

Perhaps this is to be expected. Several years ago, Carey McWilliams, then editor of the *Nation*, observed that investigative reporting occurs in cycles. About every 15 to 20 years, he said, there is vigorous activity, which trails off only to return several years later. Although there is always some investigative reporting going on somewhere in the country, I believe that McWilliams was right in saying that its popularity waxes and wanes with the mood of the country and, quite possibly, with the type and degrees of corruption that investigations reveal, whether in government or in the private sector.

But, generally, investigative reporting has thrived in periods of reform and upheaval. In quieter, less reformist times, the public hasn't been very receptive to revelations about improprieties. Or, at the least, such revelations seem to lack the impact they have had at other times and, perhaps which they might well deserve.

At the nation's journalism schools and on the staffs of student newspapers, investigative reporting in the IRE sense of the term does seem to be in ill repute. For investigative reporting in the IRE sense means that reporters examine, through their own initiative and work, an issue or problem that the public needs to know about but that someone, for whatever reason, has concealed. Unfortunately, just as people can romanticize those who carry out this role, they can also be skeptical about it. In fact, the

AUTHOR'S NOTE: Speech delivered at the Investigative Reporters and Editors national conference, Portland, Oregon, June 28, 1986.

investigative reporter has passed from the role of folk hero in the days of Watergate to that of pariah today.

For example, in conversations with journalism students at two of the country's leading journalism schools, I found them less than sympathetic to the plight of NBC's Jim Polk, who in 1985 found himself uncomfortably entangled in national security issues. Polk had covered the Ronald Pelton spy case and in the process reported details of some of the U.S. intelligence that Pelton had been accused of selling to the Russians; this so infuriated CIA director William Casey that he formally recommended Polk's prosecution under an old but still effective federal statute governing communications intelligence. The students asked tough questions and wondered what Polk had been doing mucking around in this sensitive area in the first place. I cannot imagine many students expressing that view in Watergate days when Woodward and Bernstein were stalking that great story.

But to the students' credit, their declining interest in investigative reporting reflects more than disaffection with a romantic image of the investigative reporter; it represents mostly a recognition of the diminished importance of government and thus public affairs reporting in our society. Some of the students said to me, "Ronald Reagan has all but dismantled the government, what with deregulation and all. Aren't these government-exposure stories really less important than analyses of business and economics?" One student put it bluntly: "A lot of investigative reporting chases after penny-ante local scandals. I wonder how many reporters worry about some trivial expenditure by a fire chief while they ignore a story of much larger impact in corporate offices across the street?" Of course, it is not exclusively an either-or question; vigilant coverage of government is vital to our democracy, but I, too, have wondered if stories that are in the end quite trivial don't sometimes outdistance coverage of the private sector, which also needs high-quality surveillance.

Part of the declining interest in investigative reporting of government can be linked to the rise of business journalism. There we have seen real gains, and, while some of this work is not truly investigative, it is analytical and does dig deeply into how various corporate strategies will affect the public. Here, however, probing public records will uncover only a small part of the story.

After an initial flurry of interest a few years ago, many journalism schools have settled back into their old patterns, and rarely do we see them adding investigative reporting courses. Some professors will argue that all reporting is essentially investigative, but, unless investigation itself gets special attention, there is little coherent development. The need for a course specifically dedicated to investigative journalism is evident.

As those who believe investigative reporting to be an important contribution to the craft of journalism see this approach decline further, the role of the journalism school as a nurturing beacon may be especially important to investigative reporting's survival.

The interest in investigative reporting that does exist in our journalism schools is quite strong. Work of high quality is being done. Teachers devoted to this approach conduct useful courses and seminars and also do research pertinent to understanding the critical relationship between reporting and public policy. Investigative reporting underscores that relationship and is a useful method of instruction for news gathering and writing. Indeed, the important "paper-trail" work of IRE is a superb example of systematic information gathering in an era when public records and documents can be linked through data bases to a broad range of sources that can truly give perspective and meaning to a journalistic report.

Universities can help keep investigative reporting alive not as a professional calling in exile, but as a vital force for American journalism by teaching students the strategies and tactics of this approach. They can showcase the best examples from print and broadcast journalism and also suggest alternative approaches that could have reached the same results. Universities can also conduct research on the shape and contours of investigative journalism, looking specifically at how to improve its information-gathering methods. For example, a person who is skilled at using the new databases to collect information might have suggestions for reporters who are either not thinking very deeply about using these resources or who are not likely to go beyond the field of journalism looking for ways to adapt them to their use. When it comes to the effective use and quality control of databases, journalism schools can take a broader view, looking to other fields, such as computer science and sociology, for examples.

What this suggests is a shared interest between journalism educators and investigative reporters. They can be allies in improving and expanding investigative journalism at a time when the professional and commercial world doubts its value. They can also advance and elevate this vital enterprise reporting by adding new knowledge through research and by providing a steady flow of students who appreciate its value and contributions to their craft.

Pulitzers and Other News Prizes

When the *National Journal* challenged the originality of Pulitzer prize-winning work in *The Philadelphia Inquirer* in 1988 (and was joined by *Harper's*) the public got a rare if oblique view of the Pulitzer process. The dispute recalled similar complaints spoken and unspoken over the years, and although a special committee of the Pulitzer board quickly adjudicated the complaint—and found no basis for revoking the *Inquirer's* prize—its inquiry raises several questions worth exploring.

The Pulitzer judges do their job if they impartially assess and evaluate the work submitted by American newspapers seeking this coveted honor. With scores of entries, they must work with dispatch; there is little time to research the originality of each entry or to determine whether someone in another medium might have covered the story first.

Of course, the Pulitzers aren't alone when it comes to complaints about the appropriateness and fairness of the honors they confer. Other much-sought after awards in other media and in allied fields also spark debate by those who feel that they did the ground-breaking work on which a prize-winning entry was based.

Still, the debate is not without merit. As long as we take Pulitzers and other prizes seriously as indices of excellence, they will generate controversy. People will ask whether the honored work is really the best work, and they will ask about the process itself, wherein many interested parties serve as jurors and board members.

Moreover, this might be the time to ask whether medium-specific awards really mean very much in an integrated information society. After all, news is covered and developed by print and broadcast media, by cable and various specialized magazines and data bases. When one honors only newspapers, it is certainly possible to single-out work that, in fact, has been bested by a magazine or a network newscast.

The great news scoop that led to the Iran-*contra* scandal, for example, came from *Al Shirra*, a Lebanese magazine. It, of course, was not eligible for either a Pulitzer or a National Magazine Award, which raises another, related question: Do insular national awards given to a single medium make any sense in a modern media society? If they do, it goes without saying that much original and perhaps seminal work will go unrewarded while derivative reports reap the honors.

AUTHOR'S NOTE: This essay appeared originally in the May 1988 issue of *Communique*, the newsletter of the Gannett Center for Media Studies.

The most recent Pulitzer flap introduces once again the matter of attribution. Last year when Senator Joseph Biden paraphrased and appropriated the speeches of another politician, he was roundly excoriated by the news media for his lack of character. Yet it is not uncommon for reporters to lift ideas, concepts, and especially words and phrases from their sources and from other media. And it is rare that they give credit.

This, in fact, was one of the alleged sins of *The Philadelphia Inquirer*, which might have simply acknowledged the earlier efforts of the *National Journal*. Of course, resourceful reporters read and research extensively as they prepare material for a general audience; typically they are not encouraged (or expected) to deal in heavy attribution. Now it seems that this practice ought to be modified, at least to some slight degree.

There was a time during the newspaper wars of the 19th century when it was unthinkable to give credit to a competitor, and, until fairly recently, newspapers and the electronic media did one another few favors when it came to recognizing competing work. This is changing slowly however, and it is no longer a badge of shame to cite sources, even when they are competitors. Still, this is more the exception than the rule.

While not every story can be fully sourced for the public, major series and especially important accounts ought to let the public in on sources, both original and secondary, such as other publications, reports, documents, and books.

Nobel laureates don't lose their standing when they praise the contributions of predecessors, colleagues and collaborators whose early efforts made their own triumphs possible. Journalists should take a step toward professional maturity and follow this excellent example.

Health News and Its Consequences

Journalism educator Hillier Krieghbaum called me one morning in March 1988, to talk about health and the mass media. He said he had determined that AIDS is one of the most ubiquitous news stories of all time. "How do you know?," I asked, and he responded, "It made the real estate page in the *Times* this morning!"

Kreighbaum, who has tracked media coverage of health, medicine, and science for several decades, had offered a keen observation. Not only has coverage of AIDS commanded enormous attention in the press for several years now, but it has also crossed every boundary and subdivision of news coverage.

News about AIDS is now so complex, so ubiquitous that its consequences for the media are just beginning to be considered. A few years ago some public health experts could rightly complain that the story, once described as an obscure "gay cancer," got scant attention, but now some of them worry whether it is getting too much. They also worry about the quality and nature of that coverage, as explosive headlines and debate attended the recent pronouncements by Masters and Johnson.

There are few areas where media interests and societal interests have coincided with a body of research that can be as instructive as the current preoccupation, even fascination, with health coverage, largely stimulated by the AIDS story.

For nearly 50 years social researchers concerned with the consequences of messages and media on individuals and society have charted the course (and impact) of communication campaigns. Many of these have dealt with health and health issues, asking whether good health practices can be promoted and influenced by information. The results of this work have been mixed, contributing to the continuing debate over whether the media have little effects, big effects, or no effects at all.

As the distinguished researcher Everett Rogers of the Annenberg School at the University of Southern California said, it all depends on one's expectations for the message, health or otherwise, on the intended audience.

Rogers and William McGuire (of Yale) are cautious about making great claims for the health message. Again, though, the case of AIDS is instructive, for rarely has knowledge about a disease and its consequences spread more swiftly throughout the population. There is evidence that information

AUTHOR'S NOTE: This essay was first published in the April 1988 issue of *Communique*, the newsletter of the Gannett Center for Media Studies.

delivered by the press through other educational/informational efforts is having an impact on not only people's health practices, but their behavior as well.

At the moment, many in media see themselves as "health educators," disseminating information that will inhibit spread of the disease. While some worry that contemporary health news is alarmist or misleading, most of it has tread a responsible line between scientific caution and the noisier debate of public policy. Clearly, there are many actors in the drama, many self-interested parties (some of which certainly also have the public interest in mind) that will disagree.

For these reasons and others the media need to steer an independent and professionally sensitive course so that they do not become captives of any singular interest. Unlike other major news stories, however, coverage of health can benefit enormously by what is known about the "consequences" of communication on this topic. Few other news topics have been so thoroughly studied by first-rate scholars who have a good sense about how the public gets and "processes" information.

The modern health story is the subject of massive, continuing coverage, and public understanding of and response to that story are vital intelligence for responsible reporters and editors. Happily, the marriage of research and professional practice can and should benefit us all.

Sports: the Serious and the Celebratory

Although sports may seem inconsequential when compared with the economy, foreign policy, and domestic politics, such a narrow view ignores an important point: Sports and the media are mutually dependent institutions. Although both had truly independent origins, their overlapping relationships now make it hard to imagine one without the other.

The media without sports would lose an enormous amount of their advertising revenue, as well as a significant percentage of programming content in television and of the space allocated for news in daily newspapers. Sports, by the same token, have reshaped themselves to please the media audience; they need media revenues for survival, and they depend on print and broadcast coverage to give their people and organizations identity and credibility.

The workings of the mass media as they encounter sports are multi-faceted. Sports are at once news, opinion, entertainment, and advertising. Sports as pure entertainment capture the human condition, making heroes of both individuals and teams and functioning as a showcase of national pride. This aspect of the media-sports connection is replete with lively sportscasters and other media "cheerleaders" who enthusiastically celebrate sports as a metaphor for life itself.

But the media also regard sports in a very serious manner. A look at the bottom line for media-and-sports revenues makes clear the importance of this symbiotic relationship.

Those who monitor the sports-media connection often confront the serious and the celebratory aspects of the relationship between these two mighty institutions. No one doubts the power of sports as profit centers because of their near universal appeal to viewers and readers. The rationale that trims time off the *CBS Evening News* to accommodate the final minutes of a tennis match clearly gives sports a priority over news, although some would argue that this, too, is news. And it was no accident that when *USA Today*, with the benefit of market research, began publication five years ago, it contained a large and impressive sports section, one that harnessed technology to audience interests.

In this quite serious mix is sportswriting, the best and worst of American journalism. No subject covered by the American media generates a greater range of stylistic quality and substantive information. Sports journalism can

AUTHOR'S NOTE: This essay first appeared in the November 1987 issue of *Communique*, the newsletter of the Gannett Center for Media Studies.

take the form of investigative reports or cheerful features that promote local teams and players. Some sports journalists see themselves as reporters first and sports experts second; others would reverse the order.

Although critical sports journalism is nothing new (tracing its origin at least to the "Black Sox" scandal of 1919), there has been a tension in the development of sports journalism since the 1970s that involves comprehensive coverage of "the game" as well as coverage of "the problem," and thereby likely to include labor disputes between owners and players, drug use, homosexuality, racial tension, and other issues.

Whether and to what extent media involvement with sports reflects values stimulates much debate. Because sports are linked to sportsmanship and such "end states" as "fair play" and "egalitarianism," they often get more intense scrutiny than other social institutions.

Blacks broke the color barrier in baseball before they did in most of the rest of society, initiating a debate about racism that continues to this day. Similarly, the eminent place of sports in education, from grade schools to universities, is a statement of values. Sports have been critical to the identity of many colleges and universities in the United States, for example, in principled and unprincipled ways.

In spite of the many complex contours of the media-sports relationship, the topic per se is not often tackled in a serious-minded fashion by media commentators, scholars, and critics. While the substantive "stuff" of sports gets plenty of analysis, the sport-media-money connection, sports journalism and other links between these two vital institutions often get cursory comment or none at all.

I cast my vote with those who believe that sports are not just games, but a vital concern that touches many aspects of life, from economics and entertainment to law and medicine. And, at the same time, it is vital to understand the celebratory, joyful aspect of this important topic. While acknowledging "joy in Mudville," sports have a deeper dimension worthy of intelligent commentary, criticism, and analysis.

References

Elliott, Deni, ed. 1986. *Responsible Journalism.* Beverly Hills: Sage.

Fishman, Mark. 1980. *Manufacturing the News.* Austin: University of Texas Press.

Goldstein, Tom. 1985. *News at any Cost: How Journalists Compromise Their Ethics to Shape the News.* New York: Simon and Schuster.

Merrill, John C., and Odell, Jack S. 1983. *Philosophy and Journalism.* New York: Longman.

Schiller, Dan. 1981. *Objectivity and the News: The Public and the Rise of Commercial Journalism.* Philadelphia: University of Pennsylvania Press.

Schudson, Michael. 1978. *Discovering the News: A Social History of American Newspapers.* New York: Basic Books.

Stephens, Mitchell. 1988. *A History of News.* New York: Viking.

Weiss, Carol H., and Eleanor Singer. 1988. *Reporting of Social Science in the National Media.* New York: Russell Sage Foundation.

Figure 6.1
SOURCE: Jim Morin - *Miami Herald*. Reprinted with special permission of King Features Syndicate, Inc.

6

Under the Microscope: Media Scholars and Critics

It Wouldn't Work in Theory: Overcoming
Resistance to Research About the Mass Media

Not long ago, a distinguished economist visited several of the world's great corporations. He talked with executives and managers and observed people at work. On his return to the university, he remarked that what he had seen might work in practice, but that it certainly wouldn't work in theory!

For more than 50 years now, industry researchers and scholars in universities have studied, probed, and analyzed the mass media. They have inventoried their range and scope, tried to determine how much impact and influence particular messages and particular media have on their audiences. And they have also given us a close-up outsider's portrait of how media organizations work — and who makes them work. While there is no great mystery about any of this research, some of it, such as studies of where people get their news (TV's triumphs over newspapers), is well known; while others (such as the role of editors as gatekeepers) sometimes seem rather arcane.

Research about the mass media comes in two streams: one of them quite public, the other proprietary. Proprietary research, carried out by commer-

AUTHOR'S NOTE: The 1986 Edward Clissold Lecture, Graduate School of Journalism, University of Western Ontario.

cial firms or in-house researchers for particular newspaper or television stations is typically only available to those who pay for it. Public research is generally the product of academics or government researchers and is yours for the asking.

Beyond this distinction, however, research also comes in at least two other forms, basic and applied. Applied research is problem-solution research that probes for practical results. For example, research on circulation at daily newspapers is applied research, designed to tell the paper's management who is no longer subscribing to and thus reading the paper. Acting on such findings, a paper might revitalize or add a section, with new content and a new look, in order to attract new readers or rekindle the interest of old ones. This is precisely what the *Toronto Star* did in its hometown competitive battle. Most media research is, as the *Star*'s was, applied research.

Basic or theoretical research is more abstract, often has no immediate utility, but is designed to foster understanding, as it might for the processes of communication. For example, some early research on message transmission in news organizations is of real value only in the abstract.

Now what does all this have to do with the rough-and-tumble business of print and broadcast journalism?

If you had never been inside a newspaper or broadcast station and only knew about them from theoretical treatises on their operations, you would probably agree that there is a great gap between theory and practice. For a variety of reasons, the yield of research about mass media does not always jibe with the personal experiences of people who work in the field. Indeed, what one sees in practice does not always find its way into theoretical formulations or even into individual pieces of research about media issues and problems. This leads many professionals to the conclusion that media or journalism research is simply so much nonsense, with little — if any — value. I have witnessed meetings of editors and broadcasters where the tables of contents of leading academic journals were read aloud for their comical effect. Certainly a central question for media scholars and professionals is whether research and theory about the mass media can be valuable, particularly in an information age in which other industries are benefiting from research and development while we lag behind.

On several occasions, I have observed Fred W. Friendly's Socratic dialogues with journalists. Invariably, Mr. Friendly (or one of his hired inquisitors) will ask a journalist to explain his way out of a hypothetical ethical dilemma. "What did you do, then?" Friendly asks, and the journalist responds quite confidently and succinctly. And then Friendly inquires, "Why? *On what theory?*" Here the journalist looks puzzled, confused. Then comes the response, typically a convenient rationalization, often inconsistent with the previous explanation.

Not surprisingly, journalists appearing on Mr. Friendly's panels often appear to be random and unthinking when compared with lawyers or other professionals. Lawyers, for example, have theories, but journalists don't seem to. Journalists are fond of talking about "situational ethics," and about "changing conditions," but the idea of an ethical imperative or a thoughtful store of knowledge against which to weigh decisions is quite foreign to them.

There has been no universally accepted base of knowledge that all journalists or media professionals must have in order to do their jobs, although, I think, this is rapidly changing. There is more common ground available for understanding media than most critics admit, but perhaps not yet enough to warrant claims that a genuine theory exists. What is a theory?

Once, when he was trying to explain an exhibit of modern art, critic Hilton Kramer complained that some art seemed to lack a persuasive theory. "And given the nature of our intellectual commerce," Kramer said, " . . . to lack a persuasive theory is to lack something crucial — the means by which our experience of individual works is joined to our understanding of the values they signify."

Theory and research are the conceptual tools by which we stand back from the singular experience of individual situations and make some general conclusions. You will never see trends that affect media coming from the vantage point of a single newsroom, but, with the experiences of many, it may be possible to see the larger issues, the turbulent twists and contours, the sea changes.

While anti-intellectual practitioners are fond of bashing research, whether it's generated in commercial firms or universities, leaders of the communication industry do in fact rely more and more on the evidence of first-rate research to make marketing decisions. They do so because the media are changing, and changing rather radically. They do so in an effort to survive against competitive forces. They are getting smart about research, knowing that information about their audiences is crucial to positioning even a general-circulation newspaper in its community.

No longer, for example, can editors plead ignorance of market penetration, of relative competition from other media, or of specific information about the nature of those moving targets they call their audiences. All this is connected with selling advertising or finding other kinds of economic support for media enterprises. Once it was possible to claim that the audience and the community were one and the same. But not any more. New technologies are challenging the old order, and those who want to survive in this rigorous climate had better start singing "What a Friend We Have in Theory."

There is no better example of this development than the commercial broadcasting enterprise in the United States. For years, the networks called the tune. They not only provided programming for the nation and owned some powerful stations, but they had wide political and economic influence. It used to be said that a network president in the United States was like a cross between a Supreme Court justice and a college president. No longer. Now, as one congressional staffer told me recently, they are like any other "self-serving businessmen petitioning Congress for favors." What accounts for this striking contrast, one that has occurred so swiftly as to have gone unnoticed? The answer, economists say, is found in the challenge of new technologies and in the inevitable forces of market segmentation. Life itself was changing, and so did television.

A few weeks ago, in the midst of the corporate upheaval at CBS in New York, press critics at first focused on the gossipy details, trying to make the event a human drama. When the dust settled, however, it seemed less a drama than the result of inexorable economic currents that required all broadcast content — including the news — to be profitable. What had happened to news at CBS had already happened a few years before to American newspapers, which responded to changing technology and changing economic conditions by studying both their audiences and their potential audiences. Then they boldly redesigned themselves, recalibrated their content, and made efforts to recapture and extend their audiences.

Commercial research that probes the audience for obvious economic reasons is here to stay. Media companies will pay for it, and it will be used both as an offensive and a defensive tool. However, a close look at commercial research, some of it of the highest technical quality, demonstrates conclusively why it is also limited, why it is insufficient both for the media and for society. To begin with, proprietary research is just that: "hired-gun" research done to meet the client's specifications, much as an architect might work for a builder. In the United States at least, newspapers, magazines, network television, and radio typically sponsor most of the industry-wide research. There is very little high-quality cable research. Each research vendor (and some well-placed industry research organizations) have a mandate to "prove" that a particular medium is more effective than another and thus preferable as an advertising vehicle. Thus the television industry tries to show why advertising on television is better than advertising in newspapers, and so one. Every member of the media family engages in this defensive research effort, and the information it generates is presumed to be of great value to those who commission it. Clearly the media must think it valuable, or why would they pay so much for it?

Curiously, advertisers and ad agencies that spend hundreds of billions annually in the media pay just a fraction of the cost of ratings and other research, and are seldom willing to spend more to improve its quality. Some research has much less immediate utility, and thus media organizations ignore it or support it at a quite niggardly level. For example, news research which can help in the news-gathering process and can actually make media more responsive to the public, gets relatively little support. Similarly, media organizations rarely do research on personnel, the people who comprise the media. And only in the context of sales do they do research on the comparative positioning of media against one another.

While industry support for communications research in universities in the United States is still quite modest, it is experiencing an incremental acceleration, a welcome development to anyone who cares about the public consequences of our communication. In recent years, foundations, government agencies, and media companies have funded research that has probed the impact of television on children; the role of violence in the mass media; the attitudes of the public toward the news media; print and broadcasting treatment of minorities and women; coverage of business, education, politics, the military, and other specialized concerns. There has even been a thoughtful and systematic look inside media organizations, offering new evidence about the nature and attitudes of the people news organizations employ, management problems and patterns, means for the public to respond to media, and a variety of legal issues, including libel and privacy.

With this support, we are close to having a respectable corpus of scholarship that will identify great issues and from which we can draw conceptual maps or theories. Much of the media research done in the past has had a dead-hand tone or has simply measured performance. It has rarely been prescriptive, truly analytical, or forward-looking. Now that is changing.

Within the last two years, Americans have had something of an obsession with credibility research. Several major industry organizations, the American Society of Newspaper Editors, the Associated Press Managing Editors Association, the *Los Angeles Times*, and the Times Mirror Corporation, all conducted and released major studies. Most acknowledged a major credibility gulf separating the press and the public. And most of them followed up on their research with specific recommendations that would make newspapers and broadcast stations more responsible to their audiences. These studies, while finding many of the same things, did not speak with one voice. The Times Mirror studies, which were given wide visibility courtesy of major newspaper and magazine ads, took issue with the idea that three-fourths of all Americans had a problem with the credibility of the media, saying that when credibility was defined as believability the press got much better marks.

But the studies had another value. They placed the mass media in the context of other social institutions, including business, government, and the courts. And they took the temperature.

Now, armed with the best intelligence ever available on this subject, American editors and broadcast executives are finding creative ways to monitor their own performance and make their organizations more pertinent and more accountable. Why are they doing this? For benevolent, Lady Bountiful reasons? Not at all. Because freedom of expression is in jeopardy (a condition pointed out by a lack of public confidence in the media and an increasing number of libel suits) and for economic reasons, cultivating public confidence and support will play a large part in determining which media survive and which ones are buried beneath corporate tombstones by their competitors.

Ironically, while it is possible to cite fresh new examples where university research, both basic and applied, has had substantial value to the media industries, there is nothing new about this process. Again, in the United States, broadcasting has traditionally been the most-researched medium. That research begun in industry, was further developed in the universities, and spawned modern marketing research and such artifacts of survey research as broadcast ratings. Much of today's research in the tradition of the ratings suffers from an arteriosclerotic aging process and badly needs an infusion of new ideas.

Like White Knights to the rescue, a number of young scholars, most of them in universities, are challenging the traditional approach to research, asking that there be more qualitative analysis and less bean-counting. They wonder whether the method of research itself doesn't frequently bias the answers, and whether media research should always genuflect to the communications industries.

I believe that there is room for wide-ranging research that employs different methods to ferret out answers. Certainly empirical efforts to scope out and measure the audience and its reactions have proven their worth. But so have historical and legal analyses, as well as literary examinations of media issues and problems. Some research rightly probes the nature and purposes of mass communication. Other efforts look at the impact and influence of communication on individuals, industry, and society itself.

This research focuses on the impact of mass communication on the audience, but there is also research that concerns itself with the impact of the audience on mass communication. There is research that looks inside media organizations to see how they are structured and why, who their employees are and what they do.

In the midst of the credibility studies, for example, came a book called *The American Journalist.* The first major study of U.S. journalists and their attitudes, the book provided a valuable profile of who journalists are, what they think, what their educations are like, what their aspirations are, and more. One of the book's most profound findings was that there is a very high drop-out rate in this youth-oriented field, a finding that has obvious value to media industries and society. For it points out a major personnel problem — and a very costly one — for media organizations. In such a snapshot of research, then, we can identify a problem that cries out for a solution.

Still other media research and commentary can properly be called criticism and analysis. It sometimes comes from outside the media family and from critics who would change the nature of news coverage or the content of entertainment programs. All this is a natural consequence in a communication society.

Anyone who looks at the history of mass communication research is struck by several levels of development and some evidence of maturity. Still, it seems to me that there is really a paucity of research and no agreed-upon, coherent theory of mass communication.

In an era when bankers, lawyers, and other interests are invading the communication industry, when the very nature of communication is being constantly redefined, I believe there cannot be too much research, especially research of high quality that asks important questions and seeks coherent answers. In an information society, even the smallest enterprise needs to be research-minded. The weekly newspaper, for example, may not be able to carry out sophisticated research, but it can be an intelligent user of available information, and it can benefit greatly from the public research, often conducted by universities, that provides a pathway amid the darkness and confusion of information pollution and unyielding economic upheaval and competition. For example, Ruth Clark's research for the Newspaper Research Project identified several reasons why young people don't read newspapers, information that many editors found very valuable in reacquainting that audience with their papers.

Media research and theory can be sense-makers, and, while almost all research has some value, that produced at universities is less likely to be either adversarial or self-serving for any particular medium and so is potentially of great social value. Moreover, university-based research often cuts across more than one medium and so is less susceptible to myopic introspection, in part also because it uses a variety of approaches and methodologies.

But research costs money, and university budgets usually have paltry sums devoted to this purpose. Thus it seems incumbent upon those interested in sociotype that can benefit most from high-quality media research to support it. To me that means the mass media: the print and broadcast organizations that are the central nervous system of our system of social communication. It also means private foundations and, in some instances, government agencies. Remember that all funding agencies have agendas and that no research is ever completely objective or totally impartial, so we must support a variety of research efforts.

But what sorts of efforts? What can be done to unite industry's resources with university-based research, research that can have either immediate or long-term value for the media and the people? What can the communications industries, and especially the news media, do?

First, provide support. Give money. Clearly money talks, and high-quality research costs money. Contribute to individual university research programs or join, even modestly, in joint research efforts with other newspapers or broadcasters.

Second, consider joint media-university research enterprises. Do this by keeping university researchers, especially those at journalism and mass communication schools, informed about major issues and problems that need practical solutions. Maintain a dialogue with university researchers. Invite them to your organization.

Third, ask for research interns. In addition to interns who do editing and reporting chores, consider taking on graduate students for short-term assignments, either in advertising or news research.

These kinds of support will lead to diversity in research and much-needed interaction and debate between all the parties who care about public communication. We can and must learn from each other. In the end, perhaps, we can agree that theory is more beautiful, more perfect, than practice because it teaches lessons that take us beyond our own experience and allows us to share that of others. Perhaps, then, we will have what the writer Tom Wolfe has described as theories that were "more than theories." As he put it, "They were more than theories, they were mental constructs. No more than that even, . . . veritable edifices behind the eyeballs, they were . . . castles in the cortex. . . ."

No, the newsrooms of North America may not work in theory, but in their collective practice is the stuff of which theories are based and which will enhance and elevate the nature of mass communication itself.

Recovering the Media's Lost Legacy

When Richard Kluger's elegant examination of the late *New York Herald Tribune* (*The Paper: The Life and Death of the New York Herald Tribune*, published by Knopf, 1986) recently made its way to the best-seller list and won high praise from critics, it reminded us once again that the media have a history. And in that history is substance that helps us know and understand what mass communication is all about.

Some people react with dazzled amazement when a book about the media gets genuine public attention. That they should do so strikes me as curious.

But perhaps for the same reason that physicians don't spend much time thinking about medical history, many media people are oblivious not only to their profession's history, but also to sources of intelligence about its present and probable future.

Recently, when a New Hampshire court pondered the enduring question of whether reporting is a profession, journalism's insecure sense of itself as a field worthy of examination and analysis emerged again. Predictably, some commentators argued that journalism has no accumulated body of knowledge and therefore was not a profession.

Intelligent and informed people, however, cannot seriously entertain this argument. For the press as well as the rest of the media do have an accumulated substantive literature.

Anyone who assembles a communication library is struck by the range, scope, and power of that literature. Not only is there an orderly and impressive history of the field, the work of media scholars and professional historians, but there is a growing organizational and sociological literature as well.

Studies assessing the impact and influence of the media and other communication are numerous, while internal analysis of media organizations and their economic underpinnings, a more recent and more fragile development, is growing. Also expanding is a philosophical literature concerning ethics and mass communication. Media-government relations are the subject of hundreds of studies stretching back more than 100 years, and added to that is the wealth of literature on the law of mass communication.

One of the joys of any look into media and communication scholarship is its ready acceptance of different ways of knowing.

AUTHOR'S NOTE: This essay first appeared in the January 1987 issue of *Communique*, the newsletter of the Gannett Center for Media Studies.

It has been open to the methods of documentary scholars from law, history, and literary studies as well as the methods of social scientists. Qualitative assessments from the emerging critical studies movement add yet another useful dimension.

Although media studies draw on many scholarly traditions and methods, it has also achieved an identity of its own, independent of any one discipline or professional perspective. And yet as the media and mass communication have become central to society, a proposition that almost everyone accepts, there is little agreement about who in the academy should monitor, examine, and analyze media behavior and influences.

Although they still have not gotten full recognition, the communication and journalism schools are in the first rank of those who care deeply about media matters and engage in serious scholarship and criticism. Close behind are social scientists and historians who find media studies a useful means to other ends.

Increasingly, media critics and those who cover the media as an institution are also paying more attention to the accumulated, if not fully accepted, literature of the field.

While they sometimes forget to consult this accumulated wisdom (for example, during the present Iran-arms controversy) in their more reflective moments they are drawing on the lessons of historical analysis and social science to explain the context of press-government relations, the libel litigation crisis, the uses of the media by advertisers and much, much more.

Much of the media and journalism's legacy is lost because it hasn't been properly retrieved or made palatable for a caring audience. Whether it involves patterns of media ownership or the impact of new communication technology, there are contemporary lessons in much of the accumulated and accumulating literature of media studies.

At present the yield of this scholarship has relatively few takers. Only a minority in the journalism schools are genuine producers or users of such evidence about mass communication, and other academics have only a tangential interest.

The public, it seems to me, has much to benefit from access to this unheralded intelligence. If the media are playing a central role in society, and I think they are, then perhaps educational institutions from the secondary schools to the colleges ought to integrate some aspects of media studies into their curricula.

Precisely how this happens doesn't matter much. What does matter is that intelligent and educated citizens have systematic information with which to

Figure 6.2 Mike Peters — Dayton Daily News/United Features Syndicate
SOURCE: Reprinted by permission of UFS, Inc.

navigate in a media-intense society. When that happens, a book like Richard Kluger's will not be treated as an anomaly, but as a satisfying taste of intellectually stimulating discourse of considerable importance.

Whence We Came: Discovering the History
of Mass Communication Research

Communication researchers almost instinctively look toward the future. As they study the impact and influence of the mass media, they are caught up in a fast-paced, continuously changing world. Whether these researchers work in industry, for media organizations, or in universities, they monitor and investigate such highly competitive and fluid phenomena as newspapers, broadcast stations, and other communication enterprises.

What is now called communication research or, often, media studies, began in the late nineteenth century with literary, legal, and historical inquiries about the press. By the 1920s sociologists had discovered this field and enriched it with institutional analyses. By the 1930s audience researchers, coming largely from the new field of broadcasting, added their imprint to the intelligence about mass communication. They did this in collaboration with leading social scientists from the universities: sociologists, psychologists, and political scientists. The field of media studies grew quickly, spurred by industrial development, wartime propaganda efforts, and the advent of high technology.

By the 1970s, communication research was a thriving enterprise that, while dominated by social scientists and their empirical methods, also engaged documentary historians and legal scholars, as well as popular culturists. While it would be difficult to argue that the field came of age then, it was at least well anchored by graduate programs, research institutes, and a growing literature. Communication research even came to play a modest role in the formulation of public policy on public television, children's programming, violence, pornography, and other issues.

There was little time for reflection during the formative years. Communication research was an enterprise on the move, looking for new research questions, seeking funds, and positioning itself to address the great social questions. Occasionally, leading scholars would assay the state of communication research, but these early examinations were little more than literature reviews, syntheses of recent research with marginal connections to earlier work, most of which appeared in annual reviews of psychology, social psychology, and communication.

AUTHOR'S NOTE: This article was originally published in *Communications Research: The Challenge of the Information Age*, Nancy Weatherly Sharp, ed., (Syracuse, N.Y.: Syracuse University Press, 1988), pp. 3 - 20. Used by permission of the publisher.

As long as communication research remained on the periphery of such other disciplines as sociology, social psychology, and political science, scholars had no compelling reason to give much thought to its history. But, as media research developed its own niche, there came to be more reasons to wonder about origins.

The earliest work in what can now be called "media studies" was decidedly qualitative. It was descriptive or analytical, sometimes drawing on the methods of historical research or literary criticism. It was systematic work of a humanistic sort. By the 1940s, however, quantification was in vogue and communication study emulated the world of science more than that of literature or history. To be sure, there were always historians of the press, communication law scholars, and cultural essayists who did research, but the empirical scholars were in the spotlight and generally held sway. By the late 1970s this preeminence was challenged by qualitative researchers, many with an ideological bent, who decried quantification and questioned the utility and value of the prevailing research tradition. This conflict and controversy inadvertently ignited interest in the history of mass communication research.

What has resulted is a lively inquiry into the origins and growth of this important, multi-faceted field. This contemporary preoccupation with the roots of communication research is coincident with a self-conscious assessment that asks whether we in the field know what we are talking about and whether 50 to 75 years of scholarship add up to anything useful or pertinent.

Knowing and understanding what mass communication can and cannot do has become a high stakes game. And, because communication research is or should be the locus for answers to compelling questions of theoretical and practical value in an age of information, the history of the field has come under the scrutiny of thoughtful people in industry and the academy. The current debate revolves around young researchers involved in cutting-edge public policy issues, audience-analysis people at the major networks, and representatives of major media research organizations who do workaday studies for newspapers, broadcast stations and cable companies. The debate that seemed to begin in the footnotes of academic journals now engages not only professors of communication but major players in the media.

A series of seminars at the Gannett Center of Media Studies at Columbia University in 1985 and 1986 provided one indication of the significance of this "history of research" debate. When organizing what we called a study group on the topic, we invited a variety of university and industry people to attend. They did and were asked to bring along colleagues and students. At one meeting, vice presidents for research from three national networks attended because they thought the inquiry was important. The study group featured presentations by major figures in the field: Frank Stanton, the former CBS president and a pioneer in broadcast research; Wilbur Schramm, founder of four communication research institutes and the most widely published scholar in the field; Robert W. Merton, internationally known sociologist and a founding father of communication research; Kurt Lang, expert on the European origins of media research; James Carey, cultural critic on communication and a leader in the field; and George Gerbner, also a gifted editor and critic.

When someone asked Frank Stanton if he had been the first researcher in American broadcasting, he responded, "Oh my, no. Mal Beville was already at NBC, and there were others." Hugh M. Beville, the man mentioned, attended the next seminar. Then 80, he had published a new book on audience research in 1984. Faculty members from Columbia and nearby schools attended regularly. Others commuted from Philadelphia, Washington, and the Midwest. By their presence they were saying, "This is important and worth my time." The yield of the Columbia seminar was several major papers and hours of lively dialogue wherein the beginnings of communication research were debated and discussed. Who were the founders? What were their intentions? Why did they pursue particular questions? Who paid for the research and why? These and other questions inevitably came back to a seminal concern: What do we know about mass communication and the mass media? The Gannett-Columbia study group was concurrent with interest elsewhere in the country in the history of communication research and what has been referred to as the "rewriting" of that history.

Writing or "Rewriting" the History

To speak of "rewriting" the history of communication research suggests that there is an orthodoxy codified and readily available. That is not the case. When scholars refer to the "historiography" of the field or its "received history," they are describing fragments of a complex mosaic about which there is little real agreement. That disagreement centers on when and where communication research originated, who among its founders were most influential, and other questions.

Although there is no written history as such, periodic summaries of findings and trends, as well as synthesis reports, are often referred to as the "received history." Still, there is a controversy that pits researchers with one view of the past against those seeking interpretations.

Influence of Thomas Kuhn

In a number of disciplines now reflecting on their pasts, whether glorious or not, the culprit who stimulated the critiques is a most unlikely figure, a thoughtful and measured historian of science named Thomas Kuhn. His seminal book, *The Structure of Scientific Revolutions*, published in 1962 by the University of Chicago Press, seemingly more than any other single source has fostered debate about the evolution and development of knowledge. The field of mass communication is no exception. Scholars considering the emergence of scientific knowledge about communication find concepts of change advanced by Kuhn — change by exception, incremental change, pendulum change, and paradigm collapse — a compelling framework for analysis.

Paradigm change involves a major reassessment of the way researchers have structured and, thus, have understood knowledge. That concept was on sociologist Todd Gitlin's mind in 1978 when he wrote a blistering critique of the "dominant paradigm" of mass communication research. He attacked the quantitative traditions of the master surveyor, Paul Lazarsfeld, and work initiated in Columbia University's Bureau of Applied Social Research. He saw Lazarsfeld and others who studied media effects with empirical methods as mere "administrative researchers" who were servants of industry bound up by "intellectual, ideological and institutional commitments."

The resulting controversy has centered on the "relative importance" of the mass media in comparison with other social institutions and influences on people's attitudes and behavior. The so-called minimal effects theory of media impact and influence identified with Lazarsfeld irked Gitlin, who wrote scathingly:

> By its methodology, media sociology [mass communication research] has highlighted the recalcitrance of audiences, their resistance to media- generated messages, and not their dependency, their acquiescence, their gullibility. It has looked to "effects" of broadcast programming in specifically behaviorist fashion, defining "effects" so narrowly, microscopically, and directly as to make it very likely that survey studies could only show slight "effect" at most. It has enshrined these short run effects as "measures" of "importance" largely because these "effects" are measurable in a strict, replicable, behavioral sense, thereby deflecting attention of larger social meanings of mass media production.

A number of commentators fired return salvos for, after all, the paradigm collapse critique not only challenged much of modern academic research but also such durable industry research as broadcast ratings and newspaper readership studies. Thus, commercial researchers quickly joined in the reassessment of appropriate ways to measure attitudes and opinions to determine whether media messages could bring cognitive, attitudinal, and behavioral changes.

Quite naturally, this fostered historically oriented defenses by those in the "minimal effects" tradition. It was not unusual in the late 1970s to see leading television researchers, for example, rise at scholarly meetings to defend the underlying assumptions of their work (and that of their mentors, especially Lazarsfeld). This reinforced research aimed at cognitive considerations that used such labels as "agenda-setting," "coorientation," "uses and gratifications," and others, as Donald Lewis Shaw and Maxwell McCombs have written.

Progression of Interpretations

Not all of the efforts to sort out the historical development of mass communication have been associated with critiques of the so-called "dominant paradigm" of minimal effects. Some commentary has been much more matter-of-fact, even benign. Several books have attempted to organize systematic evidence about the field of mass communication along the lines of media power. The thesis advanced in these books is that there has been a progression of interpretations, generally described as the *powerful, minimal,* and *return to powerful effects* schools of thought.

In this understanding of the field, early studies based mostly on impressionistic and anecdotal analysis prior to the late 1930s reinforced the notion of a powerful press, which used a "hypodermic needle" metaphor, suggesting that the media injected information into an impressionable public. With more systematic and careful measures in the 1940s (courtesy of social science), the media seemed less powerful, and thus the term "minimal effects" was coined. In the 1960s and 1970s several researchers challenged the old order and called for a reassessment of the dominant view. The German researcher Elisabeth Noelle-Neumann spoke of "the return of a concept of powerful media effects," an idea seconded by other researchers, fostering what has been called the "big effects-little effects" debate. Although it is somewhat simplistic to characterize complex research patterns and trends with post-hoc buzz words not used by the original researchers, that is what has happened. Thus, the early period of communication research history is characterized by the "hypodermic needle" or big effects theory. It is, in this interpretation, replaced by the "two-step flow" paradigm of Elihu Katz and Paul Lazarsfeld. Anthony Smith notes that "as quickly as one kind of influence is denied, another springs into parlance." There is an apparent need to label and characterize (sometimes even to caricature) research themes and trends.

The return of "big effect" was influenced by such developments as the writings of Marshall McLuhan (suggesting television was central and pervasive), the cognitive research of Shaw and McCombs, as well as British and French scholarship on the content of media (e.g., television as a text) that led to cultural and critical studies.

Interdisciplinary Perspectives

The writings of Wilbur Schramm and Melvin De Fleur have long provided a historical explanation of mass communication research with material that blends (a) intellectual influences from various fields that have had profound impacts on communication research (e.g., learning theory) with (b) efforts by social scientists who have "tarried awhile," to use Bernard Berelson's phrase, on communication problems, and (c) the work of researchers who have made this study their exclusive scholarly preoccupation.

Historiography

Interest in the historiography of mass communication research is seen in articles by David Weaver and Richard Gray codifying the history of communications research from a journalism school perspective; Steven H. Chaffee, from a political communication view; and Byron Reeves and Ellen Wartella, as the history of effects research concerns children. James Carey has written about the cultural underpinnings of communication research, well outside the empirical tradition, and has critiqued historical research. Gertrude Robinson offers a technological explanation in a recent critique of the history of North American communication research.

There has not been much effort to trace early intellectual origins or to assess and evaluate the influences of Lord Bryce, the English traveler and observer who toured the United States in the late nineteenth century, or philosopher Walter Lippmann in a historical analysis of public opinion research. Exceptions to this are writings by Kurt Lang on the European origins of mass communication and Hanno Hardt on the German roots of social theory. Most contemporary historical reviews begin in the 1940s and rarely stretch back beyond the sociological and social-psychological roots of the field. Indeed, with few exceptions, the historical, legal, and literary work of scholars concerned about the media or freedom of expression gets little attention in current critiques, yet this work predated empirical efforts and has considerable continuity, having moved through several stages of development.

Concurrent Streams

Neither has much been written about the concurrent streams idea that we explored at Columbia in the study group. In this historical analysis, there are several concurrent streams of activity, some of them interrelated, some not. This analysis recognizes the longstanding interchange between the academy and the communications industries. What will probably always be lacking in any historical review, though, is an insider's analysis of commercial and proprietary research. Although done to assist a particular media organization at a given time, its cumulative impact is considerable, yet rarely shared outside industry circles.

The concurrent streams analysis looks at schools of thought that have influenced and guided communication research. Because communication research emerged concurrently in interrelated fashion at various universities and in governmental and industry settings, it is useful to talk about streams of activity while still recognizing that this is a simplification of something more complex. We are discussing the European origins of mass communication research, the Columbia and Chicago "schools," the rise of mass communication research in journalism schools, the war research, industry research, and the current reassessment that features several alternative viewpoints.

The Columbia School. The Columbia School includes the work of a generation of empirical researchers who have been concerned with attitude formation, as well as tools and theories of measurement and analysis. Embracing work by scholars at several universities, including Yale and Princeton, it has involved mass communication studies aimed mainly at determining the impact and effect of media messages on individuals, which, in turn, has led to the development of various theories about society and culture.

This research, largely carried out with industry and government contracts, has been eminently practical and may have influenced much of modern media marketing research. It played a major role in providing intelligence about audiences to the new and emerging radio and television industries from the 1930s through the 1950s and beyond. Preeminent in the communication capital of the country, Columbia-trained people (here I mean also those associated with the other institutions influenced by Lazarsfeld and other leading figures of the period) have taken important research jobs at the television networks and other media research organizations.

The Chicago School. Even before the Bureau of Applied Research was active at Columbia, sociologists at the University of Chicago were studying mass communication issues and problems. Under the guidance of Robert Park and others, studies at Chicago focused on problems related to the sociology of work and knowledge as well as organizational theory. This has included studies of media organizations, the nature of news, and people who work in media. Unlike the Lazarsfeld-Columbia group, the Chicago scholars have been more likely to use participant-observer methods or content analysis than survey research. At Chicago and among those influenced by its intellectual traditions, the emphasis of research has tended to be on the internal dynamics: the economics and structure of the media, the "product" of communication, and the people involved in the process.

The Communication Schools. Although research was being done in journalism schools prior to the development of formal research bureaus, such activity got an infusion of energy with the establishment of institutes or centers for communication research at Stanford University and the universities of Illinois, Wisconsin, and Minnesota in the 1940s and 1950s. These programs, under the direction of such leaders as Wilbur Schramm, Ralph Casey, and Ralph Nafziger, were lively foci for projects involving contract work for industry, but they also engaged in theory construction and methodological testing. Strongly guided by the Lazarsfeld tradition and tied to public opinion research, these programs also embraced part of the Chicago tradition since they studied media organizations and their problems. Several of the principals of the new centers assisted with war research and other policy-oriented efforts after World War II. These programs trained generations of graduate students who now staff many of the nation's schools of journalism and mass communication. Some are also in industry.

The War Research. Concurrent with the Bureau of Applied Social Research and its progeny — indeed involving some of them — was government research on propaganda conducted during World War II. People from industry and the academy were employed by the government to assist with information campaigns to test various communication styles and strategies. The assumptions of those researchers were vastly different than the ones of those who had done propaganda analysis in the 1930s and before. Much of the early work belonged to the "powerful press" school, which made many conclusions about media and power without much empirical testing or analysis. The "war research" activity was continued, in concept at least, through the 1960s and 1970s in the form of governmental commissions and other efforts to examine public problems (race relations, pornography, the effects of television, etc.). This was administrative research conducted either by government agencies or by universities under contract to solve particular policy problems.

Industry Research. Yet another element in the history of communication research is industry activity, which is often concerned with audiences and advertising. Much of this is medium-specific. Early efforts by Lazarsfeld and Stanton were used to scope out and grapple with the radio audience. Later this activity inspired a modern system of broadcast audience ratings. Efforts by Chilton Bush and others did the same for newspapers and their readership problems.

Organizations like the Magazine Publishers Association, the Newspaper Advertising Bureau, and the Television Advertising Bureau evolved and engaged in research aimed at proving that their medium was *best* for delivering a particular audience. The purpose was unabashedly self-serving: to help a particular medium (or media organization) ascertain its strengths and weaknesses with the audience in order to capture a large share and, thus, get more advertising revenue.

An ultimate outgrowth of this approach was the massive Newspaper Readership Project of the 1970s, which attempted to provide audience and potential audience data to arrest declining newspaper circulation. This study, perhaps more dramatically than any in recent history, led to the remodeling of many newspapers and to what has been called a "marketing approach" to news. Long before this, television audience research, some of it carried out by "media consultants," had reshaped television entertainment and news programs.

While these industry research efforts have reinforced traditional approaches, commercial studies have not been without critics. One critique of modern audience research was expressed at a 1984 conference at Columbia University titled "Beyond Ratings," which not surprisingly contained many of the same issues one finds in attacks on the Lazarsfeld tradition.

Evaluating the Yield of Research. Today each of the concurrent streams is being analyzed and reviewed by scholars interested in the origins of communication research. Some commentators are social scientists who want to know whether understanding past research endeavors provides clues about appropriate approaches to such studies today. Others are critical theorists applying a Marxist or neo-Marxist analysis to questions about who pays for research and why.

But, to date, only a few of these historical tracings have concerned themselves in any complete way with the intellectual "bottom line." What do we really know? In what areas has the yield of research been productive and powerful and in what areas is there a paucity of evidence?

Ironically, one of the most critical examinations of the dearth of unifying theories growing out of mass communication research came not from the "young Turks" of the field but from Schramm, who asked whether the field had "produced a central interrelated body of theory on which the practitioners of a discipline can build and unify their thinking." His answer: "I am afraid that it has not." The article appeared in an extraordinary issue of the *Journal of Communication* (Summer 1983) called "Ferment in the Field," which is by far the most comprehensive analysis of the current state of mass communication.

Field or Discipline?

There are a number of ways to sort out the meaning and yield of mass communication research, but they are often encumbered by debate over whether mass communication study is a *field* or a *discipline*. Some who argue that it is a discipline look at the process and effects communication and begin with such basic building blocks as signals, messages, and other aspects of theoretical analysis. They say that the advancement of knowledge about mass communication has now reached disciplinary status with some accepted theories and generally agreed upon assumptions. They also point to a massive literature developed by people who call themselves mass communication researchers. One proponent of this view is George Gerbner, who writes, "What makes communication a discipline is that it has something to say about every human and social situation. As do history, economics, physics or any of the established disciplines, communication has a unique contribution to make to the understanding of any human relationship or situation."

Not everyone agrees with this approach. Some who believe that mass communication is a field of study rather than a discipline, for example, compare it to international communication. It is, they say, a field or topic that can and does benefit from the work of many scholars representing a wide variety of disciplines, from political science and history to psychology, sociology, economics, American studies, and law.

The distinction between discipline and field is that in the former, mass communication is preeminent as a topic for study; in the latter, it is a subset of a scholar's primary discipline, whether politics, law, or social relations. Either approach can be effective in organizing the history of the field.

Retrospectives

There is little historical material on the evolution of mass communication as a distinct discipline, tracing the contribution of other academic disciplines or fields. Neither is there a cogent history from the point of view of any of the contributing disciplines that have brought their theories and methods to bear on media or communication problems. What we do have are annual reviews of psychology, social psychology, and other disciplines that regularly inventory the present stage of knowledge about mass communication from their points of view. One of the best on mass communication deals with media effects. Written by Donald F. Roberts and Christine M. Bachen, it appears in the *Annual Review of Psychology* (1981) and is part of a long line of such reviews.

Various yearbooks and journals collect exemplary research done during the previous year and occasionally attempt to determine the scope of the history and direction of the field. Individual subfields, such as communication history or international communication, also occasionally evaluate their present statuses with historical analyses. For example, communication law scholars have begun to critique their past as a rationale for new methods and, thus, a new perspective on old but still important problems. These and other subfield retrospectives usually have as their purpose a "past is prologue" analysis. The contours and currents of the field are examined for their pertinence to the contemporary scene. Indeed, their authors rarely think of these reports as history.

Answering Society's Questions

A truly telling review of the history of mass communication research would ask whether the major questions of society had been addressed. A cursory review might be a useful indicator of the true status of mass communication research, not just its historical contours, but the nature, dimensions, scope, and quality of its contributions.

What have mass communication researchers studied? In addition to the categories of research mentioned in annual reviews, the field has often been divided into three parts: *external* research (effects and other media-society issues); *internal* research (the inner workings of communication organizations); and media *criticism and analysis* of both.

A large and perhaps overarching concern has been media power — the impact, influence, and effect of mass communication. Scholars have not always shared common definitions or engaged in precisely comparable studies, but this has been a consistent theme in media research, and no other topic has approached it as a dominant concern. Most of the work has been empirical, has used systematic methods, and typically (but not always) has employed quantitative measures. There also has been a cultural and humanistic stream of effects research in studies of popular and mass culture. This largely literary tradition has been concerned with themes and patterns of media content or with the image of particular groups, individuals, or movements.

If the "media power" research has been largely external, concerned with the effects of media messages on individuals (or on society and culture) in an outward fashion, there has been another approach to research that has been more internally oriented. Sometimes called "media sociology," it most likely derived from the "Chicago School." This approach looks at the product of mass communication (news or entertainment, styles and standards of journalism, etc.); the nature of the organization (groups versus independents, management styles and approaches); media people (who they are, what they think and do, and what their ethics are); and other activities within organized mass communication.

Neither internal nor external research has to be self-possessed or parochial. For example, contextual comparisons of media industries with other industries are illuminating and useful. And certainly, no effects or impact research has any real meaning without the context of other influences on the individual, groups (family, school, or religion), or society itself.

A less well developed line of communication research might simply be called media criticism and analysis. Here the tools of the historian, the literary critic, and the legal scholar are useful in probing concepts (such as the public interest or the theory of representation), themes in media criticism, and other concerns. This research is typically more normative, more concerned with the exploration of problems and solutions. Most empirical research also is problem oriented, but actually finding a solution usually is not its main aim.

In recent years, the criticism and analysis of mass communication has been augmented by the work of cultural and critical theorists (many from Britain and Europe), who have not accepted the underlying assumptions of earlier work. For example, Jay Jensen's assertion that media criticism must begin with the clear recognition of the profit orientation of the media has been disputed by current critics who have challenged the existing economic order.

What Graduate Programs Tell Us

In many academic disciplines, the structure of graduate programs reflects the way knowledge is organized in the field. Typically, this is not a conceptually neat, well-ordered framework. Instead, it reflects years of turf battles by faculty members. This is also true in mass communication. In a number of leading doctoral programs, research activity is organized in a fashion that separates *substantive* topics (what is studied) from *theory and methodology* (the tools for study) in such a way that the results are somewhat confusing. For example, several programs follow the model of the University of Minnesota, which divides mass communication into four subfields: theory and methodology, history of mass communication, mass communication agencies as social institutions (media sociology and law), and international mass communication. Some of these subfields emphasize substantive topics or problems; others are process or method-oriented. This is not an anomaly at Minnesota but reflects other programs and, to some extent, the organization of the field.

Each of the subfields gives scholars "diplomatic relations" with their counterparts elsewhere. Indeed, there are "social institutions" scholars, communication historians, legal scholars, and communication theorists. A related approach is used by the Annenberg School at the University of Pennsylvania, which has a tripartite division of the field including: (1) codes and modes (the transmission of messages through various media), (2) communication behavior, and (3) communication systems and institutions. There are other formulations in other graduate programs, all reflecting a given institution's view of the field, local traditions, sources of funding, and specific interests of individual faculty members or students.

Although it can be argued that the conceptual framework of many communication graduate programs does not achieve intellectual perfection, there is an emphasis on unified areas of knowledge that cuts across all forms of communication and mass communication rather than aims narrowly at a single industry and its interests. This is both a virtue and a vice. Over the long haul, the benefits of broadly-gauged study that is generalizable from one setting to another is obvious, but in the short run — and through much of the history of mass communication research — the lack of an industry orientation by many communication schools has led media professionals to think that communication research is not pertinent to their problems. Thus, industry representatives sometimes have urged scholars to organize their programs to serve particular needs, differentiating newspaper interests from those of broadcasting or advertising or cable television. Indeed, at several universities, chairs have been established that specifically target the research needs of a given industry.

While universities welcome this kind of support and it gives them useful links with industry, such medium-specific research can encourage fragmentation in understanding the larger processes of communication. At a time when all forms of communication are coming together in an electronically-based and computer-driven system, the commonality can be lost in research programs that are organized from a newspaper, magazine, or advertising point of view. The same can be said for research that is funded by business, the health care industry, or other special interests. Business and law schools have generally managed to avoid the trap inherent in research that has as its starting point a narrow interest rather than unifying concepts. Moreover, it can be argued that such an orientation duplicates the work of media industry researchers.

Universities ought to have a different role and function. A university's ability to move beyond parochial interests is important in establishing a genuine discipline that pursues knowledge rather than specific short-term goals that make headlines in the trade press. Although this may not be responsive to the "quick fix" demands of industry, it may be more useful to industry over time because of the research and development implications that are found in theory construction and in the application of new methods of analysis.

Does Research Have Any Value?

Looking at organizational patterns of communication scholarship is useful in seeing where researchers have been. It also helps focus a vital concern: Have these researchers addressed the major questions of importance to the public in general and to those who specifically care about mass communication in America? Have the great and enduring issues been considered? And, if so, with what success? Is the research worth the effort or is it a kind of "brain bank," employing talented people who are working on irrelevant matters?

Because the history has not been written in any definitive way, there are no easy answers. What one needs is not a simplistic "bottom line" accounting but instead a conceptual map that might consume many volumes and require complex presentation. In addition, there is a need for a mapping device that helps both scholars and professionals understand the contradictions and complexities of research. Still, it is useful to hazard a look at key questions, relating them to research evidence in a spirit of hypotheses-building rather than dogmatic evaluation. Since the preeminent question — that of effects, importance, and power — has already been reviewed in this discussion, I will consider other vital matters.

On questions of freedom of expression our research literature is quite thin. There are hundreds of fragmented studies of given legal cases and concepts, many fewer on freedom of expression itself. There is little that illuminates and makes sense of competing interests and rights that come into conflict with the free flow of information. What work we do have comes mainly from the field of law and legal philosophy.

On economic questions (such as those relating to the nature and meaning of ownership patterns of the media, the role of advertising, and audience analysis) there is a very limited literature. The entire literature of the economics of mass communication is quite small, and, even though there is much current interest in media management, the field of economics has barely emerged.

On technological questions there has been, with few exceptions (including a study of the role of the telegraph), little work on the emergence of the Information Society and on the Communication Revolution. While it is incontrovertible that books and articles on subjects like cable television, direct broadcast satellites, and videotex have a limited shelf life, it is disturbing that there is so little research being generated by mass communication researchers and others with a communication orientation. There is, of course, a good deal of technological research being carried on by engineers and lawyers, but the communication field is hardly holding its own, even on questions bearing directly on media organizations and products.

On philosophical questions there is cause for some, although not a great deal of, celebration. For more than ten years, the ethics of mass communication has been a topic of central concern. There have been a number of important books and articles on media ethics. In addition, several philosophically-oriented studies of other underpinnings of mass communication have appeared. Indeed, some philosophers in mainstream philosophy departments have turned their attention to mass communication questions.

What these four foregoing summaries suggest is a need for a regular, systematic inventory of what we know and what we need to know. Such an effort would encourage scholars, industry leaders, and funding sources to put efforts where the intellectual and social pay-offs could be great.

Clients and Constituents

A review of mass communication research history gives clues about the producers of such research, whether in the academic or commercial worlds, and the motivation behind their work. Some are theory-builders or scholars more interested in the tools and measurements of research, while others are responding to substantive questions important to educators, the media industries, or the public. There has been relatively little discussion of the constituency and clientele for communication research, which is also central to understanding its history.

Who are the constituents for research and how have they influenced the shape of its history? Within the university, researchers themselves and their colleagues in journalism and communication schools are primary constituents. They have done research because they have intellectual interests in the problems to be studied and because they seek promotion and tenure in increasingly research-oriented universities. Colleagues who are not research-oriented can be secondary users of research although sometimes they are antagonists to it. Other faculty members in the university, in far-flung fields, are indirect constituents since the research enterprise of communication and journalism schools helps bring academic legitimacy. Without a perceived contribution to knowledge in a research university, faculty members and their departments suffer greatly. Students ought to be a constituency as well. They should benefit from research in their courses and contribute to it both as research assistants and as subjects of studies.

The external constituencies for communication research include media industries, government agencies, foundations, and various private organizations interested in knowing more about the media for their own priorities. They sometimes purchase, commission, and/or fund research. In recent years the output of journalism and communication schools in meeting the needs of these various organizations has seemed modest. There is considerable criticism among media industries about the lack of pertinence of communication research in the university, and funding agencies have not been overly generous in supporting projects in journalism and communication schools. Similarly, government agencies, which were frequently tapped for funds in the 1960s, no longer provide much support for mass communication efforts. Perhaps this is part of a decline of support for social research although funding for various technological projects is occurring in other fields.

Summary and Conclusions

This paper, which is intended to stimulate thought rather than answer questions, is written at a time when there is much interest in the history of mass communication research. The research archives have not heretofore been well-tended and, consequently, retrieving the history is an unfinished chore. What can be done is to sort out the patterns of activity, the schools of thought, and the pervasive interests of researchers. When that is done, it is clear that there will be a field (or discipline, take your pick) with a substantial corpus.

While there is communication research of the highest intellectual quality, the field has attracted giants, it is also true that the overall quality is not impressive and that much research is not especially rigorous. Thus, symposia of the kind organized by Syracuse University have enormous value in moving the research enterprise ahead. It can and ought to be improved and upgraded. It should get more support both in the academy and in industry, not for narrow or self-serving reasons but because this is an Information Age when the citizens' needs for understanding are high. The advancement of knowledge will help them and, in turn, society.

Remembering Wilbur Schramm

When the *New York Times* noted the death of Wilbur Schramm on its January 1, 1988, obituary page, it gave this great student of mass communication less attention than it did a local delicatessen owner.

But Wilbur Schramm would have understood that. With gentle good humor he might have talked about news with immediate and delayed rewards, something he had written about long ago.

Wilbur Schramm came to visit us in Morningside Heights in 1986 when he addressed our study group on the history of mass communication research. Dr. Schramm recalled that Columbia's master surveyor, Paul Lazarsfeld, a founding father of communication research, had encouraged him when he founded the respected Institute of Communication Research at the University of Illinois in 1948. Columbia's Robert Merton, a giant in sociology and Lazarsfeld's colleague and collaborator, was there that day, as were other leading figures in media research.

We had asked Wilbur Schramm to talk about himself that day, but he demurred, choosing to pay tribute to the other founders of communication research. Someone remarked that Schramm's appearance was symbolic, because no one has played a larger role in defining and articulating media studies. In his original work on media effects, media sociology and ethics, international communication, educational uses of television and much more, he helped organize the field.

He did so *On the Shoulders of Giants*, in the title of Robert Merton's important book, as he helped synthesize and integrate the work of others from fields like social psychology, sociology, economics, government and journalism.

When Schramm retired from Stanford University, Steven H. Chaffee remarked that if our field has a great man, "He is our great man." And Wayne Danielson made the case with specifics, noting that because of Schramm, children are reading and writing in Africa, Asia, and Latin America.

Schramm was a scholar and an institution builder. And what a life he led. As a young man he played in a major symphony and with a semi-professional baseball team, wrote "fireside chats" for Franklin Delano Roosevelt, did research for the War Department during World War II, founded the Iowa Writers Workshop, modernized the Iowa School of Journalism, created research institutes at the universities of Iowa and

AUTHOR'S NOTE: This essay originally appeared in the February 1988 issue of *Communique*, the newsletter of the Gannett Center for Media Studies.

Illinois, as well as at Stanford, and the East-West Center in Honolulu. He wrote numerous books, including *A History of Human Communication,* which carries a 1988 copyright.

Importantly, Wilbur Schramm took on urgent problems: he used powerful tools to solve them and got others to continue the work long after he had moved on to other matters. On almost any topic in communication study, he left his footprints before other scholarly travelers arrived. On several occasions in Palo Alto, Honolulu, New York, and Acapulco, I got the benefit of Wilbur Schramm's wisdom and good advice.

Once when I visited him in Honolulu, I waited for him to conclude a meeting with a delegation from Thailand that had come asking his advice about establishing a telephone system in that country.

From his conversation in which he commented on his important 1943 *Plan for the Iowa School of Journalism,* still a useful document, to his views on "the communication century," Dr. Schramm always demonstrated that he was a big thinker who knew the context of communication and understood its practical implications for media professionals, scholars, and citizens. He seemed unruffled by the anti-intellectual carping of some professionals and the angry critique of some scholars, and instead moved on, devouring new problems, offering gentle suggestions that made this vital change agent seem more like a kindly uncle.

Most media scholars are heavy users of Wilbur Schramm's great organizing principles, his scholarly output, and his instincts for institution building. No one can be a literate student of the mass media who does not know and appreciate the yield of his intellectual work. He gave our field what Tom Wolfe would call "a rocket boost of energy" and a good deal more.

References

Kluger, Richard. 1986. *The Paper: The Life and Death of the New York Herald Tribune.* New York: Knopf.

Paletz, David L. 1987. *Political Communication Research: Approaches, Studies, Assessments.* Norwood, NJ: Ablex.

Rice, Ronald E. 1984. *New Media: Communication, Research, and Technology.* Beverly Hills: Sage.

Rogers, Everett M. 1986. *Communication Technology: The New Media in Society.* New York: Free Press.

Sharp, Nancy W., ed. 1988. *Communications Research: The Challenge of the Information Age.* Syracuse: Syracuse University Press.

Stempel, Guido and Bruce Westley. 1989. *Research Methods in Mass Communication/2.* Engelwood, NJ: Prentice-Hall.

Williams, Frederick. 1982. *Measuring the Information Society.* Newbury Park, CA: Sage.

Figure 7.1

Robert E. Lee on Traveller. As president of Washington College (now Washington and Lee University) in Lexington, Virginia, Lee wrote his board of trustees in 1869: "I beg leave to submit for your consideration . . . (a) proposition recommending the institution of 50 scholarships for young men proposing to make journalism their profession."

What was the industry's response?

"I cannot see how it (journalism education) could be made serviceable," wrote Frederic Hudson, the managing director of *The New York Herald.* "The only place where one can learn to be a journalist is in a great newspaper office."

SOURCE: Reprinted by permission of Washington and Lee University.
Photograph by Matthew Miley (Michael Miley Collection, Washington and Lee University, Lexington, VA).

7

Educating Media Professionals

Educating the Educated About Mass Media

To say that the communications media are central to the functioning of our society is to state the obvious. However, American undergraduate education almost completely ignores the study of mass communications. Unless students major in communications, journalism, or media studies, they can go through college without acquiring more than fragmentary knowledge about mass communication. Non-majors who want a more coherent understanding of the subject have to engage in an academic scavenger hunt, typically beginning with an American government course.

In an effort to discover how such courses treat the mass media, I looked through more than 30 introductory American government textbooks. With some exceptions, the texts suggest that the media have only a marginal effect on American political life, an idea that dates back to the 1940s, or they offer a Marxist analysis of the media's capitalistic instincts. While I did find a more contemporary treatment of the media's effects on society in a few books, these are clearly exceptions.

The message that mass communications have only a peripheral influence on society has until recently predominated in academe, even in schools of journalism and communications. In the last decade or so, however, several studies have been made by social scientists reassessing the role of the media

AUTHOR'S NOTE: A shorter version of this essay was first published in the *Chronicle of Higher Education*, 1987, February 4, and is reprinted with permission.

in modern-day America. The dominant view now is that the media are a powerful force in our society.

Among academics, however, the all-too-common attitude is that media and communication issues are not worthy of scholarly pursuit. That attitude is demonstrated by the second-class status generally assigned by universities to media studies, whether in individual courses or full-fledged departments.

Some schools of journalism have abdicated their scholarly role, but others have become genuine leaders in research focusing on the influence of the mass media, the internal operations of media organizations, and social criticism of communication. Some researchers — communication theorists, historians, and social scientists among them — are devoting their energies to the study of mass media. However, the valuable information the research has produced has generally not been well received in academe or integrated into college courses.

Nevertheless, change is in the air. A lively media-studies movement is prompting universities to organize modern communication and journalism schools, usually out of former departments of journalism, speech, radio-television, or film studies. Perhaps more important, emphasis on advanced study is evident in several new or reconstituted institutions.

In 1947, the Hutchins Commission on a Free and Responsible Press called for "centers for advanced study of mass communication," but not until 1985, when the Gannett Center for Media Studies was established at Columbia University, did that recommendation become a reality. Since then, Harvard University has organized the Barone Center for Press, Politics, and Public Policy. Northwestern University is forming a Center for Modern Communication, and there are stirrings at the Smithsonian Institution in Washington, where a media-studies program may emerge in the Woodrow Wilson International Center for Scholars.

Whether all those programs will in fact become institutes for advanced study is not yet known, but they are proof positive that, at last, study of mass communication is on the agenda and is getting both moral and financial support.

In addition, the two Annenberg Schools of Communication, at the University of Pennsylvania and the University of Southern California, have innovative programs that were created for today's information society, not constituted from former schools of journalism.

Increasing numbers of scholars are engaging in research on mass communication, and their work has resulted in a boom in books on the subject. For the American undergraduate, however, those developments have not meant increased exposure to the nature and nuances of mass communication. This is not only unfortunate but incredible, since there are natural places for media studies in the college and university curriculum: in English, political science, sociology, history, American studies and other fields that examine the forces that make society work.

In a few instances these fields do recognize the importance and even centrality of mass communication, acknowledging its presence and sometimes even its vital role. In the main, though, media studies are ignored. The result is an educated population that is being told implicitly and by benign neglect that there isn't much to mass communication after all, or that anything one needs to know can be learned from experience.

Yogi Berra's dictum that "You can observe a lot just by watching," notwithstanding, I believe there are great lessons both of experience and of systematic research capable of giving us a better and more intelligent understanding of the media, news, entertainment, and the rest.

Universities should give considerable thought to a media studies movement, not to establish new courses and departments or to build unnecessary empires, but to make an imprint on the minds of faculty members and students in other ways, to make this concern a vital part of the academic enterprise. With the help of knowledgeable scholars and media professionals, a consciousness raising effort can be successful.

Although student-consumers would soon make such courses profitable, the principal reason for establishing them is that the study of communication is important to our society. Moreover, the literature that already exists on the subject warrants serious attention in academe.

Knowledge is the survival kit that a college education gives students to help them make their way in society. Courses that provide an understanding of communication should surely be an essential part of that kit.

Whatever Happened to Marse Robert's Dream?
The Dilemma of American Journalism Education

The occasion was elegant by any standard. The guest list numbered leaders of government and industry, media moguls, prominent intellectuals, diplomats, and educators. Sommeliers uncorked an array of fine European wines. Waiters served roast suckling pig for the main course. An elaborate dessert flambé consummated the meal. This princely scenario, which unfolded in Rome in the summer of 1985, probably holds the record for incongruity as an event "recognizing" the "importance" of journalism education. Such lavish receptions are normally reserved for the rich and powerful. Instead, the guests of honor, 10 men and one woman, presided over modest enterprises of questionable influence. They were deans of U.S. journalism schools.

"This could never have happened in America," said one guest. Two prominent members of the American delegation, Osborn Elliot of Columbia's Graduate School of Journalism and George Gerbner of the University of Pennsylvania's Annenberg School of Communication, were stunned by the Rome dinner. "I think," said one dean, "something got lost in the cultural translation. Do you suppose they think we are U.S. Senators?"

The Italians imagined they were honoring "double count" luminaries in the media profession and in the academy. While some members of the U.S. delegation possessed this distinction, most did not. Back in America, most journalism school deans lead enterprises of low status and limited influence. They are pariahs in not one, but two sectors of society.

Journalism schools are "the Rodney Dangerfields of higher education — they don't get no respect," says *Newsweek*'s Jerrold Footlick. No one challenges the position of law and medicine in society, or the corresponding status of law and medical schools in universities. But a yawning chasm separates journalism schools from the industries they serve. American journalism education, while highly regarded and even lionized in other countries, is beset by problems in its own backyard. The reason? There is no consensus about what journalism education is or should be, or even whether it should exist at all. Unlike business schools, with the coherent (some would say lockstep) curricula and clear purpose, journalism schools appear fragmented and irresolute. Young people seeking journalism schools to provide the best pathway to a journalism career is the subject of constant

AUTHOR'S NOTE: This article was orginally published in the spring 1988 issue of the *Gannett Center Journal*, "The Making of Journalists."

debate among media executives, university administrators, and journalism schools themselves.

If the public wants and deserves reliable news, it has every right to be concerned about who works in the mass media and how they are trained. At a time when society depends for its values as much on the media as on the traditional pillars of family, church and school, we ought to care about the educational development of media professionals just as we care about public school teachers, police officers, and health care workers.

It does matter how competent media professionals are, and whether or not they have a sense of ethics. But citizens not privy to industry shop-talk rarely know anything about the qualifications and standards of the people who command this country's most public forum. And the fact that the education and training of journalists is not on the public agenda says something important about the American media. The media are our agenda-setting institution; they need little prompting when it comes to scrutinizing others. Yet they rarely discuss their own organizations, much less the educational institutions that support them.

The story of journalism education in America is a story of good intentions, weak support, irresolution, ambiguity, and even deception and hypocrisy. Many (though not all) journalism schools are neither fish nor fowl in the American university. Few of them have effectively embraced and mastered the culture of higher education, or elevated their people into top academic leadership positions. The same can be said for their role in industry. While journalism schools are a source of cheap labor for employers, they rarely lead or strongly influence the course of industry developments.

If there is a dialogue about the purposes and prospects of journalism education, it is a dialogue of the deaf. The same issues and problems have been inventoried and debated for years, yielding little agreement and much confusion. Industry leaders denounce and denigrate journalism schools at one moment and eagerly hire their graduates the next.

Though the debate about the utility of journalism education is an old one, it has recently taken on a greater sense of urgency. Clearly, if journalism schools do not do a better job of defining themselves and their role, others will do it for them. More than 88,000 undergraduate and 5,600 graduate students were enrolled in 150 journalism schools in 1986. These students are the principal source of new talent for the American mass media. A full 85 percent of all entry-level newspaper journalism hires today come directly from journalism schools. (Comparable figures for broadcasting are not tabulated.) Increasingly, journalism schools also educate and train students in other communications industry sectors, from advertising and public relations to the new technologies.

But many editors, by their own admission, prefer pure liberal arts students (even though most journalism majors take 75 percent of the courses in the liberal arts), or a trade-oriented master's degree. And most of the nation's major media look to elite educational institutions for their hires, preferring bright Ivy graduates who are already socialized into the conventions of the Northeast. Indeed, any close review of the pedigrees of their new hires reveals a bias that is both elitist and class conscious.

This posture is curious for an institution that preens itself on democratic values and diversity. Only last year, when asked by a largely student audience about academic training for journalists, ABC News *Nightline* anchor Ted Koppel said: "Journalism schools are an absolute and total waste of time. You cannot replicate true journalism — genuine pressure — in an academic setting." Koppel is only one of the most recent and most prominent examples of the hallowed tradition of media executives, editors, and anchors who like to snort and snarl at journalism schools. His predecessors include H.L. Mencken, Robert Benchley, A.J. Liebling, and Walter Lippmann.

Several acquaintances of mine (none of them journalists) once discussed how people become journalists. "I suppose," said one, "they go to journalism school." "No," said another, "I hear the best editors don't respect journalism schools." A third remarked: "Educators I know don't think journalism schools belong in universities."

As it happens, they were all right and they were all wrong. Part of the problem of journalism education, and the reason that it is not really on a par with law or business schools, is the pluralism of the press in America. There are no formally agreed-upon qualifications for entry to the profession, or even agreement (legal or otherwise) as to whether journalism is a profession, a craft, or a calling. Unlike some other countries, America does not license journalists or demand that they adhere to any particular, professional code. Journalists often cite the First Amendment as the reason why. The underlying assumption of our diverse, multi-faceted press is that any individual is a potential journalist if he or she can write, report, and function in a media organization. A few years ago, when Dr. W. Walter Menninger suggested that American journalists should be licensed, his remarks ignited a firestorm of criticism. Journalists lectured the public about the absolutely inappropriate, even unconstitutional, nature of the idea. The press had a point, but the corollary idea that the workforce in American journalism is diverse, is pure myth. One of the fruits of journalism school research has been to show that journalists in America are remarkably alike in the educational background as well as their cultural, political, and religious views. If it did have formal entry requirements and licensing, American journalism could probably not have achieved a more homogeneous workforce. Once thought to be an egalitarian field where success required a "common" touch, journalists are now acknowledged to have more in common with the sources of news than with their audience.

The Ten Myths of Journalism Education

The romantic view that a college education would contaminate the would-be journalist, who needed to know life, not books, succumbed long ago to the near-requirement that journalists possess at least an undergraduate education. Many journalists today in fact hold advanced degrees. But even though a rather extensive system of formal journalism education developed in the United States, it has never had an entirely comfortable relationship with the media. And because journalism education has had a precarious relationship with its own chief constituency, the leaders of higher education have, in turn, given it short shrift within the university.

"Rarely in my career," a university president once told me, "have media executives given me the impression that they really give a damn about the journalism school. If anything they have been its greatest critics, without offering constructive advice as to how we could improve it." He added: "Some of them are really educational elitists who like the idea of a hiring hall on campus, but at the same time make clear they don't really respect it. When leading editors tell me they prefer liberal arts graduates, I wonder why I should put more resources into the journalism school."

Journalism education's shaky status in America is due to a series of myths. Ten of the most persistent are:

(1) *Journalism students study only journalism, thus side-stepping the essence of a well-rounded education.* Definitely false. The major undergraduate journalism schools require students to take most of their work in carefully-prescribed courses across the university. Additionally, they make more of an effort to demand student literacy than other departments and faculties (though admittedly with mixed success). Law school recruiters in the 1970s discovered what many editors missed: journalism majors at strong universities received balanced liberal arts educations in an era when many liberal arts majors were allowed to specialize and to avoid instruction in writing. Journalism school deans proudly confess that their "reactionary" attitude to the Pied Pipers of education in the 1960s left their rigorous curriculum intact. The richness of the journalism major is one of the best-

kept secrets of the academy. Even in most (not all) graduate journalism programs, students take courses outside the journalism school.

(2) *All journalism schools are alike—when you've seen one you've seen them all.* Journalism schools would have much less trouble explaining themselves if this were true; in fact, journalism schools come in many flavors and sizes. Some offer theoretical media studies programs, others emphasize professional training, still others offer a mixture. There are even some centers of neo-Marxist criticism. There are undergraduate majors and at least three kinds of master's degrees, as well as doctoral programs that train researchers and teachers.

(3) *Most journalism schools have abandoned the teaching of journalism.* The student desire to study "communication" instead of journalism, or to enter careers other than those in news, has greatly changed the composition of many journalism schools. To date, however, a disproportionate amount of the faculty and curricular resources of the nation's journalism schools are devoted to news and editorial concerns.

(4) *Journalism schools are not practical.* Clearly, some are more practical than others, but journalism schools are just as often criticized for being trade schools for industry instead of intellectual centers for exploring the relationship between media and society. The best schools offer extensive internships and on-campus training opportunities in connection with course work.

(5) *Journalism has no body of knowledge.* This oft-repeated assertion reflects such colossal ignorance that it should embarrass anyone who utters it. There are libraries full of books on the history, economics, sociology, politics, and the craft of journalism. There is a vast literature of media studies, both from the academy and from industry researchers. There is a vast legal and regulatory literature as well as material on international communication and other topics. With scores of scholarly and professional journals now in the field, the literature in this country and abroad is almost impossible to fathom, let alone master. The quality of this work, however, is mixed, uneven and much in need of informed criticism.

(6) *Journalism educators don't know what they are talking about.* To be sure, some probably don't. Most, however, meet higher standards than many others in the academy. At the most respected schools, the typical journalism educator has several years of professional experience and an advanced degree, usually a Ph.D. in mass communication or a related field. Faculty members who get promoted typically contribute to scholarship by doing research, writing books, and engaging in consultations with industry. It is true that relatively few (there are some) journalism professors have held high

level jobs with major media, but the same can be said for law and business professors in their respective fields.

(7) *The journalism school curriculum is simple-minded and anti-intellectual.* No doubt many courses are just that ("how-to" mechanical tricks) but many others offer advanced study of the nuances and intricacies of communication law and ethics, or of the complexities of public opinion and the history of journalism. While craft courses remain at some institutions, most schools are now in the main current of communication studies.

(8) *Journalism schools are too trendy, too willing to succumb to passing media fancies.* Most journalism schools are, if anything, positively reactionary and unwilling to change at all. Curricular reform has been slow. Some schools have failed to acknowledge or integrate new knowledge about communication. Others ignore the realities of the technological revolution in Luddite fashion, and have not adjusted their programs to the contours of the communication industry today.

(9) *Journalism schools do not attract the brightest students.* The suggestion that journalism majors rank below the intellectual average is simply untrue. From the S.A.T. to the G.R.E., journalism majors fare well above average in U.S. universities. At many schools, journalism is one of the hardest-grading departments. Journalism students are often elected to Phi Beta Kappa and other honor societies. They also get a respectable share of Rhodes scholarships, Fulbrights, Marshalls, and other awards. Liberal arts professors who openly scorn journalism schools are usually warm in their praise of journalism school students as smart and literate.

(10) *Journalism school graduates don't get jobs with the major media.* This myth would seem to be true from the comments of many executives at national newspapers, newsmagazines, and networks. But look again. While many big media companies do not hire directly from journalism schools, they all have large numbers of journalism school graduates on their staffs. They may not know it, however, because their employees were hired from other media organizations. A few major media companies do recruit directly from journalism schools, notably *The Wall Street Journal,* which has been a strong supporter of journalism education for decades.

The Origins of Journalism Education in America

Journalism schools are as old (if not as well developed) as most business, education, law, and medical schools. And, unlike some of these other professional training centers, journalism education originated in a rich intellectual tradition. Printers, the forbears of today's editors, publishers, and broadcasters were well-read leaders of public opinion. The characters one encounters in Isaiah Thomas's *History of Printing in America* or in *The Autobiography of Benjamin Franklin* were often culturally and intellectually well ahead of the lawyers and doctors of their time. Journalism has always been more than pure craft. It was often a point of entry to the literary life. The stereotype of the journalistic Philistine portrayed in *The Front Page* arrived relatively late on the scene.

The professionalization of American journalism, which started with the Penny Press in the 1830s and 1840s and culminated with the mass press of Hearst and Pulitzer in the 1890s, indirectly helped to undermine this rich intellectual tradition by instituting routine practices and a strict division of labor. The omni-competent printers of the young Republic carried out all of the mechanical, accounting, and editorial functions of their trade. Journalists were more than just informed participants in the public forum. They also knew and appreciated their own history. When Frederick Hudson's *Journalism in the United States from 1690 to 1872* was published in 1873, reviews in the New York press displayed a refined understanding of journalism history. Some critics reached back to ancient China to help put the work in context. This kind of self-conscious intellectual voyaging is rarely to be found today, even in the *New York Review of Books*. When new books in the field of journalism history are published, like Richard Kluger's *The Paper,* they are usually reviewed in a vacuum, without critical reference to other histories and biographies.

Just how journalism veered away from its intellectual roots and became, by the turn of the century, a rather rakish trade is the topic of considerable historical speculation. Some historians blame the telegraph, which encouraged short, truncated reports in the place of earlier, more expansive essays. Others point to the excesses of Yellow Journalism in the 1880s and 1890s, or to sensationalism run amok. The development of journalism into a nationally-based, mass industry, however, went hand-in-hand with a loss of institutional memory; and journalism education in the American university has yet to fill the void.

The formal origins of journalism education were in 1869, at Washington College (now Washington and Lee) in Virginia. Newspapers — the South's instruments of public opinion — had been decimated in the Civil War, and Robert E. Lee — the defeated commander of the Southern armies — had an idea that journalism should be an integral part of the rebuilding of the shattered South. In Lee's reshaped classical academy, "Press Scholarships" for students intending to make a career in journalism were offered at Washington College, alongside newly-instituted schools of law and business.

Although the program at Washington and Lee died out a few years after its pragmatic birth, journalism education could not have had a more elegant and eloquent advocate than Lee, who served as the college's president until his death. Lee's experiment prefigured other forerunners of today's schools at Kansas State College, Cornell University, the University of Pennsylvania's Wharton School of Business, and the University of Missouri. Before long, the idea that journalism education deserved a permanent place in the university took root at land grant colleges, and in the late 19th and early 20th century Iowa, Illinois, Kansas, Wisconsin, and Illinois all established programs for the education of journalists. This year marks the diamond jubilee of the national organization of journalism school professors and administrators. Columbia's journalism school, sometimes regarded as the citadel of the field, also celebrated its 75th anniversary in 1988, joining several schools which have already done so.

The Changing Columbia Model

The publisher Joseph Pulitzer had a dream of creating a journalism school. "My idea," he wrote in 1902, "is to recognize that journalism is, or ought to be, one of the great and intellectual professions; to encourage, elevate and educate in a practical way the present, and still more, future members of that profession, exactly as if it were the profession of law or medicine." Pulitzer fired off a series of letters and memoranda to advisers and to university presidents, often dictating them from his yacht on the East River, that called for the development of a journalism school. When he offered to pay for it, the Columbia School of Journalism was born.

Pulitzer preferred Columbia to Harvard or Yale because of its New York location, but he would have settled for any of the three. Columbia in fact outfoxed Harvard in convincing Pulitzer to endow the school on Morningside Heights: Harvard's President Charles William Eliot was slow to respond to Pulitzer's soundings; and when he did, he somewhat perversely (in the light of later history) proposed a trade school with courses in advertising, circulation, and typesetting. A program similar to the one proposed by Eliot was later organized at the University of Missouri. Meanwhile, Columbia's Nicholas Murray Butler had staked a claim on Pulitzer's idea and his money.

Columbia, the only Ivy League institution with a journalism school today, has played a critical role in the development of the field, largely because of its prominence in the media capital of America. Its school began as an undergraduate program with high-minded ideals, pledging allegiance not to the newspaper industry, but the "public interest."

But in 1935, Columbia declared itself a Graduate School of Journalism, and served notice that it would only accept students who had already received a bachelor's degree, preferably in the liberal arts. This decision was quite unusual for the time (many law schools did not then require a B.A. degree). In fact, it was a kind of educational "bait-and-switch" scheme. Calling itself a "graduate school," Columbia began offering a fifth year of the same kinds of courses that would later be taken by undergraduates in journalism schools elsewhere. As other journalism graduate programs developed, they followed lines more common in graduate education generally, with scholarly theory and method courses in addition to practical, industry-oriented courses. The graduate student at Illinois or, later, Stanford received "conceptual" courses and rigorous training in research. At Columbia, students typically acquired just professional and craft skills.

In a sense, Columbia's switch to graduate status in 1935 unwittingly retarded the intellectual development of the field. With just a single year of instruction, Columbia (and other schools that subsequently followed its model) played a less and less active role in generating new knowledge about journalism and communication. The intellectual center of journalism education shifted to the Middle West, where the land grant colleges forged their own traditions, cut off from the Northeastern centers of the media industry. However, Columbia did play an important role in setting journalistic standards with its high-profile program of Pulitzer Prizes and other awards. In time, scholars in other fields at Columbia (notably sociology, history, business, and law) also established a separate tradition of media scholarship, most notably in the work of Paul Lazarsfeld and his colleagues at the Institute of Applied Social Research, where modern broadcast ratings and practical audience research were born.

The Harvard Non-Model

While Columbia pioneered in many areas of journalism education, from international reporting to science journalism, Harvard has remained ambivalent over the years. Many Harvard undergraduates have progressed from the *Crimson* into media jobs, but the connection has remained tenuous and informal. After early enthusiasm for Pulitzer's idea (and, presumably, money), Harvard and such early starters as Penn and Cornell pulled back. None established journalism schools, and most joined in the chorus that scorned formal professional education for journalists as being incompatible with the aims of higher education.

The Harvard connection or, rather, the lack of it, is intriguing and probably symbolic of journalism education's difficult struggle. Until the 1930s, when a bequest by Lucius Nieman of *The Milwaukee Journal* created the Nieman Fellowships, Harvard was silent on this topic. If President James Bryant Conant had gotten his way, the Nieman endowment would have been used for buying newspapers for the Harvard library instead of bringing journalists to Cambridge. But not wanting to lose the Nieman money, Harvard succumbed and allowed the ink-stained wretches to take courses (mostly undergraduate) that offered the flavor of "higher" education in one hasty year. The idea of mixing seasoned, middle-aged journalists from the nation's vulgar newsrooms together with Harvard undergraduates at first seemed unsavory to Cambridge traditionalists, but under Archibald Mac-Leish (and later Louis Lyons) the Nieman program made a lasting imprint on Harvard, of which that university now is justifiably proud. Not until the 1980s, however, did Harvard formally recognize the value of a more systematic scrutiny of the press by establishing a center for press and politics at the Kennedy School of Government.

The fact that journalism and mass communication studies never got a department, let alone a school, at Harvard (or at any of the other Establishment institutions which set the agenda and determine the "respectability" for many fields) helped other universities either to reject the idea of journalism education altogether or to keep their struggling departments "down on the farm."

"I can't tell you how many times I've heard university presidents ask why they don't teach journalism at Harvard," one journalism dean told me. In time, major research universities in the Middle West, South and Far West, became international showcases of media scholarship. Leading the pack among research-oriented schools were Wisconsin, Minnesota, Iowa, and Illinois, while well-known professional schools emerged at Northwestern and Missouri. In the South, important schools evolved at the universities of North Carolina and Georgia, and at Emory. But most of the nation's strongest journalism schools developed far from the major newsrooms, and in the Northeast, Columbia has remained something of a lone island. This historical quirk has undoubtedly contributed to the field's lack of status with most New York-based media industry leaders.

Journalism Schools Since World War II

For many years, journalism schools had small enrollments and tiny, impoverished faculties. Said one dean: "They sucked the hind tit, and were grateful for what they got." While some programs acquired academic influence and respectability, few if any ever obtained a voice in university leadership. To my knowledge, only two journalism school deans this century have become university presidents. Not surprisingly, journalism schools also had trouble getting their faculty members tenured and promoted, and some journalism schools found themselves on the endangered species list. Well-known and respected undergraduate programs at Emory, Berkeley, and the University of California at Los Angeles, for example were abolished. Others were accused of "duplication," especially in states where neighboring schools had competing programs. Virtually no one argued that journalism schools were in any sense central to university life; most universities and colleges in the United States got along quite nicely without them, thank you. While media scholarship was generally regarded as too insignificant to merit a faculty unto itself, many universities made false starts in fields like social psychology, political science, sociology, and business. And while a national report like that of the Hutchins Commission in 1947 urged scholars and citizens to take a greater interest in mass communication and its social consequences, it paid little attention to the possibility that journalism schools might play a role in this process.

After World War II, however, and especially since the 1960s, journalism school enrollments have soared. Once-inconsequential departments became profit centers in their universities. Typically, they enrolled larger and larger numbers of students onto tiny faculties and overcrowded facilities until, in time, university administrators grudgingly increased faculty complements. Some even got new quarters. Many journalism departments requested (and got) professional school status, although the vast majority (more than 70 percent) still report to deans of their parent liberal arts colleges.

The late 1940s also saw journalism education join the professional school accreditation movement. This national program established minimum standards for schools on the "approved" list, most relating to class size, faculty qualifications, and physical plant. But the accreditation process also led to an important joint venture between higher education and the industry, especially newspapers. Academics and industry, worked together, visiting schools, evaluating them, and setting standards for the field. The accreditation system worked without much controversy until the 1970s, when, with many new programs being admitted to "the club," disagreement arose over the role of liberal arts courses in journalism education. Originally designed to train well-rounded reporters and editors, journalism schools had developed into complex centers for a wide range of professional media training. There was intense debate about educational standards, and to what extent the "article of faith" — that all undergraduate majors should take 75 percent of their course work in the liberal arts — needed to be honored. The volatility of this debate, which is not yet over, has often threatened to end the 40-year pact between educators and professionals.

Their new-found good fortune led many journalism schools to broaden their course offerings through curricular "wings" specializing in particular topics: magazine journalism, broadcasting, advertising, graphics, public relations, and photojournalism. This fragmentation of the curriculum, a sort of omnibus approach to media studies, pitted journalistic purists against the hiring needs of the media industry in its broadest sense. For instance, does the study of public relations belong in a journalism school? Concurrently, America's research universities have begun to demand that all their faculty engage in "the advancement of knowledge." It is argued (rightly, I think) that a fundamental difference exists between work done in research universities and the practical tutorial instruction offered by trade schools and junior colleges.

For journalism schools, this distinction has meant that many faculty members who regarded themselves as "journalists on loan" were asked to turn themselves into fully enfranchised scholars. The dictum that "professors publish" kept many journalism schools from having their teaching faculty promoted. Schools with strong intellectual roots had little difficulty, but "boot camp" professional training centers came in for rough times. Many professionally-oriented editor/reporter professors were denied tenure. Some schools instituted dual tracks for their faculty, while requiring unusual, however, for once-active editors and journalists to stop writing and publishing once they joined journalism faculties; and this tendency probably has hurt the internal credibility of journalism schools in the university sphere more than any other. Journalism professors have had to learn that they are educators first, and media professionals second. It has been a hard lesson, and in some cases is still unlearned.

"New" Schools and the Role of the University

By the early 1980s, journalism schools were mostly unchanged in their basic structure since the 1940s and were beginning to feel the strains of their own success. While many engaged in research, the burst of new scholarship they generated failed to work its way into the curriculum, except for survey courses and occasional graduate seminars, or to have an impact on the industry. Indeed, many professionally-oriented schools were training what could only be regarded as media-illiterate students: journalists-to-be with little knowledge of the legal, regulatory, or intellectual history of the field they were about to enter. Some faculty members defiantly stood their ground and argued that they taught *journalism*, not *about* journalism, and criticized the research of their peers as "second rate" and irrelevant to the profession. (My answer: you can't intelligently separate one from the other.) But two notable proposals for reform in the 1970s did have a lasting impact. One was an eloquent plea by James W. Carey, the dean at Illinois, for journalism school programs to take up the "university tradition" and contribute to it, rather than resisting scholarship. Another was the experimental program of media studies instituted by Malcolm MacLean at Iowa, which recognized the blurring of functions and technologies in mass communication. A lack of consensus and political savvy from its proponents helped turn the Iowa program into a stunning short-term failure, but its spirit pervades more recent initiatives like the Massachusetts Institute of Technology Media Lab and the Annenberg Schools.

Meanwhile, the media industry itself was undergoing profound changes in organization and in technology. Revolutionary new applications were taking place in news and the newsgathering process, and in media "packaging," presentation, and design. As the old barriers between print and broadcast media and between the editorial and counting house functions of media organizations broke down, few journalism schools moved with dispatch to acknowledge these changes. Some obstinately called for maintaining "traditional values" against "creeping commercialism." Others hastened to buy the hardware and software of new technologies (typically, text editing systems for newsrooms), without studying their wider consequences for the modern information worker, for the industry's organization, or for the nature of the industry "product"; that is, the newspaper, magazine, or television program. Not surprisingly, nonprofit educational institutions moved cautiously in adopting wholesale changes in their equipment and curricula. Still, most journalism schools were slow to acknowledge that they needed to begin training a new generation of students, with new capabilities and skills.

As a result, other institutions have begun to step into the "journalism education" enterprise. Scholars in a variety of fields now find it respectable to study the media. Longstanding mid-career efforts by the American Press Institute were joined by additional industry-sponsored seminars and training programs. At least 15 new fellowship programs, some in university departments other than journalism, took on the task of midcareer education. The Poynter Institute for Media Studies began offering short courses to professionals, students, and academics in writing, graphics, management, and ethics. The Annenberg Schools were established to fill in the holes in communication education. Former speech and rhetoric departments launched media studies programs, and some universities created journalism "centers," where undergraduates can study media issues and practices without actually majoring in journalism. Our own Gannett Center for Media Studies was launched in large part because of the failure of anyone else to organize advanced study beyond the graduate school level and to build bridges between academics and professionals of the highest caliber. To be sure, journalism schools continue to play the largest role in the field, but their future is far from assured. The new kids on the block appear in many instances to be stealing their thunder. Ideally, these new enterprises will act collaboratively to enhance the status of journalism education on all campuses.

Several years ago, I led a project on the future of journalism and mass communication education which inventoried problems in the field and proposed model curricula. This project, funded by the Northwest Area and Gannett Foundations and loosely connected to the Association for Education in Journalism and Mass Communication (AEJMC), produced a report that suggested some ways out of what, in an impolitic moment, I called journalism education's "dismal state." The Oregon Report (as it was later called) consulted all of the nation's journalism schools (93 percent responded), industry leaders, and leading scholars. The response from all sides proved that the topic of journalism education was still a very hot potato. The report pointed out evident failings of journalism schools in a supportive manner, and suggested new approaches to strengthen the enterprise. When the dust had settled, the report's basic finding was this: the mass media are central to our society, yet because their study is hardly central in most American universities, even those with large journalism or communication faculties, the majority of our most highly educated citizens leave the university as media illiterates. The report urged journalism schools to take the commanding heights of the field, and to help not only journalism school students, but students in other departments too.

The Oregon Report coincided with sweeping reforms at a number of journalism schools. The University of Minnesota had just developed a pacesetting media studies program that cut across several different media and connected craft and concept. New schools of communication were established at the University of Miami and Penn State. New curricula were organized at Stanford, Michigan, Washington, and Trinity. When a new president at Northwestern, Arnold Weber, asked what journalism education and media studies were contributing to its research mission, he got answers from the Medill School of Journalism and from the media studies program of the School of Speech; and Northwestern instituted a new Center for Modern Communication. Concurrently, the Smithsonian announced its intention to establish a media studies program in the respected Wilson Center for Scholars.

Notwithstanding these developments, journalism education still falls uncomfortably between two stools, the university and the industry. Neither institution yet has a strong vested interest in fostering reform. At universities where poorly-funded journalism schools draw large numbers of students and serve as academic "profit centers," change will not occur without intellectual and financial support from both internal and external sources. Some university administrations hoard journalism school endowments, and allow only a trickle to flow to their impoverished programs.

At the other extreme, the media industries for all their bluster are getting a good deal. As long they can count on a steady supply of cheap labor from journalism schools, why should it change the system? A handful of media companies and foundations generously support journalism education, but most are Uncle Scrooges. They say they don't give more because journalism education doesn't meet their standards; but it can't meet their standards as long as it lacks financial nourishment. Industry has good reason to want to hire the best and brightest employees from whatever source. But many critics of journalism schools, especially media executives who write them off as irrelevant and unworthy, send a message of discouragement to three important constituencies:

—*the most highly-motivated and interested students.* Studies show that many people motivated to pursue particular careers in high school, such as student editors, often attend journalism schools.

—*women,* who constitute more than 50 percent of journalism school enrollments. Industry executives who want to avoid hiring women would be advised to stay away from journalism schools, which welcomed women when most media companies did not.

—*minorities,* for whom many special scholarships and internships exist in journalism schools. Journalism schools were not as slow as the media industry to open their doors to minorities, and recruit members of racial and cultural minorities both as students and teachers with some success. The result: a modest tradition for minority training and placement.

The Business School Model

There is a profound danger that journalism education, too often the willing or unwitting victim, could flounder and stagnate in self-pity. This would be an undesirable outcome for the university, for the media industry, and for the country. Journalism education needs understanding, moral support, and economic incentives. More than anything, it needs to reinvent itself by building on its own considerable experience and its natural alliances. In so doing, it might learn some lessons from its successful campus neighbor: the business school.

The business school experience does not supply a precise road map for journalism schools, but there are clear parallels. Until the 1950s, American business schools had fragmented curricula and lacked respect both on campus and in industry. No one was quite sure what a business school education ought to be, and whether it was necessary or even desirable. Yet today, business schools are among the most prestigious academic units on campus. Everyone knows what an MBA entails, business school faculty members are well paid, their programs are well-funded, and their students are in great demand. Moreover, business schools are also respected for scholarship and for contributions to knowledge. Industry leaders look to them for leadership and for high level advice and consultation. (Many business school deans and professors are directors of major companies, but I know of only two such instances in journalism education.)

Business school reform was instituted in response to two major studies sponsored by the Carnegie and Ford Foundations in 1959. Boris Yavitz, professor and former dean of the Columbia Business School, recalls the sudden shift in the climate: "The major schools decided to make changes to become mainly graduate programs, to attract first rate researchers and to listen to people at the highest levels of industry as they rebuilt." Business school educators faced a dilemma familiar to journalism educators in dealing with industry, according to Yavitz. "The big shots said, 'give us people with an understanding of business and society, people with the big picture, with a grounding in theory,' 'but the recruiters who came to the campus to hire asked our students, 'what technical skills do you have?'"

Instead of celebrating fragmentation and seeking to serve industry needs regardless of long-term considerations, business schools took a bold step. They decided to produce leaders for the long haul, not narrow specialists. They closed down many of their industry-specific programs, became mostly graduate schools, and began producing broadly-trained graduates, capable of leadership.

In spite of its successes, and there are many, journalism education is running at least 20 years behind business schools in terms of institutional development. If journalism schools stay as they are, they are unlikely to wither and die. But many of the educational functions they might have served will be usurped by other institutions. For journalism education to become a leading player in the modern information society, it must change. And for change to take place, dynamic thought and action are required simultaneously from three main constituencies: the journalism schools themselves, the universities of which they are a part (including those without journalism schools), and the media.

While there are both philosophical and practical reasons for journalism education to change, the incentive for change is most likely to come from the constituency most passionately devoted to and involved with journalism education itself, the nation's journalism professors and administrators. They have the strongest vested interest in improving their own enterprise. In the short run, that will require attracting more respect and more fiscal resources from universities and from industry. For this, America's journalism schools must hold their heads high and demonstrate their value, providing not just a steady stream of entry-level professionals, but also high-quality research about the media and for interested social constituencies of all kinds.

Journalism education or, more broadly, education about mass communication in general should ideally serve as the institutional memory of journalism for the media industry and the public. If they follow the lead of law and business schools in promoting a theoretical understanding of major issues and problems, journalism schools can become professional problem-solvers and public sense-makers. There is still time for them to become the architects of the information society rather than their own chief mourners. The leaders for higher education and of industry — university presidents and trustees, newspaper owners and network financiers — ought to nurture and help guide this enterprise. It is up to journalism educators to give them a compelling reason to organize support for the reinvention of this field and its place in American life.

Continuing the Search for Leadership

When the fourth Leadership Institute for Journalism and Mass Communication Education convenes here later this month, conversations will inevitably turn to a familiar topic: the apparent paucity of people available to lead the nation's journalism and communication schools.

At this writing, more than 20 leading programs are either concluding, engaged in, or planning a search for a dean, director, or chair to head their educational enterprise. Schools and departments on the list this year have included Columbia, the University of California at Berkeley, the University of Southern California, Pennsylvania, Washington, Illinois and California State at Fullerton. Missouri and Syracuse, among others, are about to begin searches for new deans.

The large and growing number of openings in these administrative posts is a problem complicated by bureaucratic search processes, few eager candidates, and many other factors. It is not uncommon for leading schools to take two, sometimes three years to find a dean or director.

In the midst of this "crisis of leadership," our Leadership Institute convenes with two avowed purposes. The first is to provide a service to new and incumbent deans as they focus their attention on three components of their task: intellectual, academic, and professional leadership. The second is to openly encourage possible future administrators from education and industry, urging them to take a fresh look at the important challenges of leading the educational enterprise that prepares America's communicators.

When universities engage in protracted searches for deans, incredulous industry people often ask why.

On the debit side of the ledger they see relatively unattractive posts wherein deans, directors and chairs preside over warring faculties, manage threadbare budgets, and do battle with critical professionals. A closer look reveals weak university support and an inconsistent pattern of financial help from industry. Add to this generally modest salaries, few perquisites, and little administrative help.

A more sanguine view, however, underscores the importance of these administrative posts in schools that are charged with a task the public should care a great deal about: the nature, quality, and ethics of the journalists and

---

AUTHOR'S NOTE: This essay first appeared in the June 1988 issue of *Communique*, the newsletter of the Gannett Center for Media Studies.

other communicators who command our public forums. There is also a franchise to lead, interact with, and redirect various intellectual resources toward the very real problems of the media and society.

The best administrators not only represent their colleagues and schools at the provost's table, but also take on university-wide leadership assignments as we enter an age of information.

They act as ambassadors to the media industries, in exemplary cases connecting them with knowledge generated in the university and opening pathways whereby their students are recruited for the best possible jobs and careers.

They also talk to one another, to their peers at other schools in this country and abroad, and thus collectively lead a field of study and professional preparation.

In spite of these worthy objectives, there is still little consensus about what qualities and competencies ideal administrators should have, or even whether they ought to come from the academy or industry.

In fact they come from both sources, yet neither the universities nor the media industries really do much to encourage this passage.

The prevailing university ethic values faculty achievement in research and teaching (and rightly so) over managerial success, but fails to provide incentives for faculty members to take up administrative assignments. Many industry people look upon these posts as the capstone of a career or a retirement billet. They are neither, since they require vision, energy, hard work, and endless patience.

What we need, I believe, is much more commitment at a national level in higher education and in the media industries to help identify, encourage, and recruit people with a passion for professionalism and the quest for knowledge that will elevate and improve our mass media.

While at the Gannett Center this month, Leadership Institute participants will meet with university presidents, provosts, financial officers, and other administrators, as well as with scholars and media executives.

Over the past three years the presence of this distinguished "faculty," most of whom are only tangentially concerned with journalism and communication, has been an encouraging indication that the task of leadership in our field is not only worthy of those dedicated to this task, but for society as well.

In time, we hope that the Leadership Institute can contribute to greater public awareness of the proper education and training of society's communicators, whether they are engaged in the media industries or elsewhere.

Education for the Information Society

The education and training of journalists and other mass communication professionals frequently stir controversy in both the academic community and the communications industry. It is a curious debate, with much of its focus on a basic question: Should journalism education exist at all? There are those in the academy and in the media industries who seriously doubt its value and say so with blunt force. At the same time, the nation's journalism and mass communication schools are well established, with large enrollments that are virtual profit centers for their respective universities. And the media, for all the protestations, rely heavily on journalism schools for their personnel. Still, the debate continues.

Much of the criticism of journalism education centers on what is taught, the qualifications of the faculty, and the trade-offs between professional education and liberal arts education. And, in the 1980s, yet another element was added to the debate: How should journalism and mass communication schools address the changing nature of the information society? While it was clear that the communication industry was coming together into a single information field guided by electronically based, computer-driven forces, journalism schools were slow to respond to this communication revolution.

Because we are in the midst of a communication revolution, which brings with it sweeping change, the need for us to also change or respond to change has never been more apparent or more urgent. So often we identify the information society, which was heralded by a revolution in communication technology, with microprocessors, satellites, and computers when it is that and so much more.

What we are experiencing today alters the very structure of our thinking and many of our assumptions about society. Thus, any change that we contemplate in journalism and mass communication education ought to emphasize ideas over machines. We are well counseled by T.S. Eliot, who plaintively asked, "Where is the wisdom we have lost in knowledge? . . . Where is the knowledge we have lost in information?" It is a question worth considering when we examine our field, which began as basic training for newspaper reporters three quarters of a century ago but is now a comprehensive system of communication studies. Appropriately, this is a time when our

AUTHOR'S NOTE: Parts of this essay were originally included in a speech before the Association for Education in Journalism and Mass Communication, of which Everette Dennis was president in 1984 - 1985.

field is under considerable scrutiny both from external critics who question our purpose and internally, from those who argue that we should modernize to improve our present practices.

In 1984, thirty leading educators and media professionals met in Eugene, Oregon, as members of an AEJMC Task Force on the Future of Journalism and Mass Communication Education and drafted a statement that has attracted considerable attention. The task force was by no means a representative assembly. Still, its members reflected a wide range of institutions, interests, and values. In their ranks were elitists and egalitarians; professionals and theoreticians; and generic communicators and industry-specific specialists. And they were armed with data drawn from national studies that consulted many educators either personally or as representatives of their respective institutions. To some the Eugene Statement will seen innocuous because it appears to state the obvious, yet I would argue that it is invested with considerable meaning because it asserts that *mass communication is central to the function of society itself and that, accordingly, the study of mass communication ought to be central to the mission of the university.*

Now, history and government and law and business are treated as central to most any university worthy of the title, while journalism and mass communication study clearly is not. Even in situations where professional schools of journalism and mass communication do an exceptionally creditable job, they rarely provide nonmajors enough in the way of service courses to be regarded as vital to the university community, either from the standpoint of delivering knowledge to students generally, or on the basis of their contribution to the larger purposes of the university. Many of our colleagues in other fields would argue that universities can operate quite nicely, thank you, without schools of journalism or any instruction in media studies. In this post-industrial society when the importance of mass communication is almost an article of faith, this seems quite preposterous. But then universities change slowly, and when there is a feverish scramble for resources it is no wonder that competitive departments will not welcome change that carries with it the shifting of funds and faculty lines. And that, of course, is what this whole battle is about. Those fields that are central to higher education get considerably better treatment than those that are regarded as peripheral.

I believe that the Eugene Statement, which has been reported fully in our various publications and which is included in the Report of the Project on the Future of Journalism and Mass Communication Education, is fine as it goes, but we should remember that it only states a desirable goal without actually taking us to that end. Therefore, I hope at this convention we can begin to close the loop on the Eugene Statement by contemplating a new conceptual architecture for our field.

So much has been written about the state of journalism education lately that I will not belabor that topic here. It is clear, though, that there are some conflicting views about the general health of journalism and mass communication education. Whether we believe that the field is sterling or stagnant, most of us would probably agree that journalism and mass communication education demands some change. Remember, though, that such discussions of change need not be negative or denigrate our considerable accomplishments.

At this convention, AEJMC and its officers will necessarily engage in some cheerleading, since we are a family of sorts, but we will be negligent if we don't also offer a critique of the field and a plan to act upon it. If my presidency has had any purpose, it has been to push our organization more toward the role of change agent than that of cheerleader. If that has sometimes been misinterpreted, so be it. For a field talking to itself, re-examining its fundamental premises and attempting to assess its strengths and shortcomings, is a field that is worthy of our best efforts and energies.

Our field has several assets that are particularly notable at the dawn of this information society:

First, mass communication is generally regarded as more vital and more important than ever before in human history;

Second, new research using a variety of methods and approaches underscores the importance (in terms of impact and influence) of mass communication and its various institutions;

Third, journalism and mass communication education is on the public agenda. We're being prodded, poked, and talked about as never before. If what we do wasn't worthy no one would care;

Fourth, cooperation between journalism and mass communication education and the various communication industries is stronger than ever before in terms of both moral and financial support;

Fifth, academic institutions and disciplines heretofore uninterested in mass communication view us with hungry eyes and are developing new instructional programs and research involving media and communication study;

Finally, we have large numbers of students whose tuition makes us one of the profit centers of the modern university at a time when other fields are experiencing stagnating or declining enrollment.

While many complain that we are not well respected and are not particularly influential in the American university, all of the factors I have mentioned give us potential clout that we ought to use for the benefit of our field and our students. The assets we have add up to unique strengths for a bold initiative that will take JMC education beyond its present diminished and hollowed state to a condition that will make it the locus of pride, hope, and exalted speculation for all who care about survival in the information society, whether as information workers or consumers. I believe we must seize this time and this circumstance.

We can also play a more vital role in the American university, a role that goes beyond mere professional training for those relatively small numbers who will enter the communication industries. We can provide general instruction for thousands of others who need to know and understand communication to function effectively in society. Just as all educated Americans need to know and understand government and the private sector to navigate in society, so do they need to fully appreciate mass communication. No university I know of makes any systematic effort to see that the majority of its students (I speak here of all students, not just those in communication) are exposed to the concepts of freedom of expression, the role of mass media in politics or consumer behavior, or other vital topics. This may, in fact, be a missing link in American higher education. Is it an unrealistic dream to think we can fill this need? Is such a noble plan beyond our capabilities or traditions? Not at all. From its beginning journalism education has been concerned about the public interest. Indeed, Joseph Pulitzer's charge to Columbia University on the establishment of its journalism school was to take the high road with public purpose. As Pulitzer put it:

> In all of my planning, the chief end I had in mind was the *welfare of the Republic*. It will be the object of the College to make better journalists, who will make better newspapers, which will *better serve the public*. It will impart knowledge, not of its own sake, but to be used in *the public service*. It will try to develop character, but even that will be only a means to one supreme end — *the public good*.

I think we have fallen from that high road. It is not because we do not believe in serving the public interest or in taking a larger role in the university for the benefit of all people, but because our financial condition has caused us to defensively protect our own students, our majors, while we cut back on services to the rest of the university. In this communication revolution, I think we can reverse this position through a comprehensive program of consumer education and public service that will take us toward the goals that Pulitzer envisioned. As important as professional education is, helping to educate and inform the rest of society about our field is even more critical. We must, I think, do both. I would add, though, that neither is likely to be done well under the present arrangements with which we live in the American university.

We will not do this if we are uncomfortable house guests in our own universities, but only if we stop making excuses, if we abandon our apologetic stance, and our fear of expansive thinking. We have been cutting corners for so long that most proposals for change are usually rejected outright because they aren't feasible. The field we represent, the knowledge we have to impart, is and ought to be absolutely critical to higher education in America, and it is time that we started acting as though this were the case. In this era of limits, of economic constraints, when we accept the concept of a "steady state" university, it may seem unrealistic to abandon E.F. Schumacher's "small is beautiful" axiom and take up Daniel Burnham's credo, which urges us to "make no little plans." If we are going to be a significant force in the next century, both within our universities and within the communication industries, we must rebuild mass communication education to make it a vital center for education in the information society.

We will not do this by thinking small and rejecting change. Nor will we do this with modest incremental change or with a celebration of the status quo. Instead, I believe that we must build architecturally, with an architect's discerning eye for the way mass and space conjoin to create a solid, yet inspiring and expansive edifice. Only then will this institution be worthy of the task before it. To do this we need both institutional and individual renewal.

First, *institutional renewal.* We need, as I have stated at length elsewhere, new structural arrangements, new curricula, and a movement away from the fragmented pieces of our field toward a more generic and coherent whole. Institutional change is hard work; it is uncomfortable and unsettling. And with some fear of offending our Florida friends, we need to drain the swamp and fight the alligators at the same time. I note, of course, that this is a phrase often used by a certain journalism dean from Nebraska, where there are neither alligators nor swamps. Change will be hard coming in many universities, but with the assets mentioned earlier, I believe that it is possible in many locales where faculties want it and where they are willing to forge a tough-minded plan for their future and fight for it. It may be slow-going and tedious, but it can be done if we respect each other and capitalize on our strengths. There are many understandable reasons why we did not do this in the past. We have always been a spare, unpretentious field that thought it unseemly to expand our mandate and get the wherewithal to do it. Now, if we are to do real service to our field, we must take a quite different stance. We must aggressively and, yes, opportunistically (in the best sense) seek the resources we need to do a job that is truly central to an educated society.

Second, *individual renewal.* While the need for institutional reform is great, it cannot be accomplished without a great deal of individual renewal. Let's do this without making the mistakes of so many educational reformers who live in a cognitive world arguing about structural arrangements, organizational plans, course names, textbooks, and other paraphernalia without considering that education is the product of people working together. People must always precede programs, and without people our JMC schools and departments are only hollow words on paper in turgid university catalogs.

Individual renewal means a new initiative to recruit, promote, and retain the best faculties drawn from the academy and from industry. It means reaching out to and providing productive courses of study for the best and brightest minds we can possibly attract to our field. The noble goal of providing both professional and consumer education for an information society is of little value if we don't elevate and advance the people in our field. We have nothing to be ashamed about in our present recruiting efforts at both the faculty and the student levels, but we must be vigilant in student recruitment and in demonstrating to bright young professionals and scholars that there is a future in journalism education, a future that is exciting and worthy of the best intellectual energies. This carries with it some assumptions about a substantial system of faculty development that encourages intellectual growth.

For too long we have been apologetic about our role and place in the university. We told our students that research showed mass communication might not be so important after all; we believed we were more peripheral than central; we accepted low status in many universities, and at the same time, we also worried about the scorn of professionals.

Now there is ample evidence that should give us a new attitude about ourselves. The elevation and advancement of our field will come only with a new view about ourselves, our role in the university and society. We need to exhibit and exude the pride that we feel in our profession, a profession dedicated to the noble purpose of educating the young (and some not so young) for a field that is compelling and alive. We ought to stop pretending we are something we are not and establish for ourselves a distinctive identity which underscores the worth of mass communication study as a discipline.

I believe we should use our abilities as communicators and scholars to develop new modes of delivering information and new methods of scholarship that will establish us as thinkers about our field in this, the information age. What I am talking about requires some national action. I believe that AEJMC can provide leadership in such a quest. We can, as we have in the last year, make proposals about model curricula and institutional reform; suggest pathways for faculty development and for student recruitment, for evaluating the quality of our work, and for coping with such social problems as racism and sexism. In the end, what I am talking about is in the preview of local faculties, of individuals who can assess their own needs and fashion a responsive plan for renewal and change.

If we are to meet our promise, major changes will be necessary. If we use the rich array of ideas at this convention, I believe we can begin to close the loop on the unfinished Eugene Statement by forging a program that will bring institutional and individual renewal. Tonight, with pride in our profession and with recognition that change can honor and elevate our earlier efforts, let's recall the words of T.S. Eliot, who told us that we must never cease from exploration and that "The end of all our exploring will be to arrive where we started and know the place for the first time."

Seizing a Special Time

Twenty years ago, the nation and the world were confronted with highly visible, dramatic changes. Some people said this was a pendulum change as we experienced massive social, cultural, and political upheaval. In journalism education there was massive growth, a broadening of curriculum interests, and a strong critical appraisal of the mass media. Today change is more subtle, sometimes so incremental that it might not be noticed at all. And yet the changes that are happening today in society and in higher education will have a profound effect on the future role and purpose of journalism education in form and fashion heretofore unimagined. It is my belief that our decisions and our planning in this field in the next four or five years may set the course for the next half century. This is a special time for all of us as we enter this information age. This is a time when universities are looking for leadership to help students and society navigate the communication revolution and the stark changes it portends. This is a special time and, in Bob Dylan's words, "It will not come again."

Let me explain by looking at two major developments in mass communication education. The first was the establishment of the journalism, and later communication, schools. They grew from programs that emphasize newspaper reporting and editing to comprehensive schools of mass communication and media studies. All this happened in the years between the early part of the century and the 1940s, when the field seemed to have achieved some maturity. While Wilbur Schramm and others had asked for broadbased and integrated schools of mass communication, their call was not immediately heeded.

Then, in the years after World War II, came a great challenge, a potential turning point for our field. It was, of course, the commercial success of television and the emergence of important questions about the place of this new medium in our lives. The journalism schools were well situated to embrace the new medium: to engage in research, and to deliver education and training, in short, to provide leadership. On this score they failed. They viewed the new medium reluctantly, even with hostility, and for the most part shrugged it off. Other university departments, then losing ground in an era when the study of rhetoric and public address seemed less compelling, did take an interest in television and electronic communication, although very often in its entertainment and production dimensions, rarely in issues of

---

AUTHOR'S NOTE: This essay was originally delivered as a speech on the retirement of Dean Albert T. Scroggins, University of South Carolina, March 1985.

news, which by default became the province of journalism education. These developments led to a fragmented, bifurcated view of electronic media that erected barriers to the holistic study of communication. Others have commented on these developments in much more detail than I could hope to here, but my reading of history is that much of journalism education failed to assume leadership for broadbased communication studies and in the process failed higher education and American society by refusing to be a major force for learning and the advancement of knowledge about mass communication in a manner useful for all citizens. Consumer education took a backseat, while professional education was proclaimed premier.

Now, once again, there is what might be a turning point in the history of communication. We are in an information age in an electronic-based, computer-driven society where the rules governing our communication system are changing and where technology and people's use of it are restructuring our concept of communication to a great degree. At a time when traditional media and narrow industry perspectives seem unable to grapple with the complexities of the blurring together of print and electronic communication, our field, journalism and mass communication, is well positioned to provide leadership. No field has a greater wherewithal not only to train media professionals, which is terribly important, but also to provide general education about mass communication to other citizens who will be media consumers.

Most educated Americans have little appreciation for freedom of expression, the transmission of information and ideas, or the media industries. While this may not have been so alarming in the past, it is today because this is a media society, a communication age when the management and control of information is absolutely central to all human endeavor. Still, this urgent problem is not being met. The nation's journalism schools cling to their traditions — honored, valued, and worthy traditions — but clearly they are capable of doing more, of making themselves and their activities a more integral part of the mainstream of higher education and the public service.

There are at least three great changes that ought to affect the development of the journalism and communication schools if they are to matter much in the years ahead. First, there is the communication revolution itself. Technology is the most visible element in a new information economy that is having an impact on manufacturing and extractive industries and changing the structure of our thinking and the way we live our lives.

Second, there is a growing recognition of the importance of mass communication. When Burke (or was it Macaulay?) spoke of a fourth estate, it was for rhetorical effect. Today mass communication is almost universally regarded as important to our politics, to our consumer behavior, and to cultural change.

Third, scholars, many who have been cautious in charting the influence and impact of mass communication, are finding new evidence of the vitality of this field. They are shifting their assessment, which used to say that mass communication had a minimal effect on human behavior, to a newer view that says that it has quite powerful effects. In spite of this evidence (and it is powerful), the hierarchy of higher education—the presidents, provosts, and deans—is not yet convinced that mass communication is important and worthy of the most serious study. Nor is the leadership of higher education willing to give the communication field a central role in the university, let alone a fair share of university resources. Change comes slow to universities, and with so many journalism schools presenting a fragmented face to their university colleagues, it is little wonder that they don't inspire confidence as genuine leaders in this information society. Remember again Dylan's words: "Keep your eyes wide open, the chance won't come again."

This is sound advice. The missed chances of the 1950s, when journalism education, research for mass communication and higher education itself lost an opportunity to be an important sense-maker for society, won't come again, but the communication revolution of the 1990s is here; and with thoughtful leadership of the kind Al Scroggins has provided, there is a chance that the study of mass communication in the context of journalism education will truly come of age. It is possible that we will see the maturing of a field, a process that will and can benefit the public interest.

As I mentioned earlier, for two years I was engaged in the Project on the Future of Journalism Education, a project that last year issued a document commonly referred to as "The Oregon Report." That report, which was the product of the collective judgment of a good many people, administrators, faculty members, media professionals, and others, provided a new vision of what journalism education might be like in the future. Its main features include a unified and integrated treatment of mass communication in the university setting. There would be a nexus of the best of professional practice and the best distrust.

In such an atmosphere a three-part program would be developed and played out. It might be shaped and driven in different ways with widely differing philosophies. But it would give students fundamental communication competency in writing, visual literacy, and information gathering. Concurrently, students would, through serious study, construct their own conceptual map of the field of mass communication. Finally, with such polished skills and conceptual understanding, they would experience calibrated professional education and training, with a recognition of present workaday realities and likely scenarios for a future beyond the status quo.

The Oregon Report outlines one approach, and there are many others, that allows for curricular planning and research development that seize upon the special character of these times in a fashion that would elevate the mission of journalism education. More than providing narrow professional training for media specialists, the communication school in this new image would truly serve the public interest.

Some people will argue that the journalism schools are not capable of this mission, that the study of mass communication is too important to be left to the communicators, just as war is too important to be left to the generals. I reject this thesis even though, at times, it is compelling; especially in the face of sluggish and unimaginative journalism education that has limited goals and a hod-carrying mentality not used to real leadership. These misgivings notwithstanding, I believe that journalism education is poised to move to the commanding heights of the communication age. At present, journalism education does not have all the necessary resources for this task.

But it does have the intellectual breadth and most of the elements necessary. Others may have technical interests and an understanding of computers and communication, but who else understands media and is committed both to the promotion of literacy and the strengthening of freedom of expression? No one is better suited or has better values for the worthy task of bringing the nation into the information age with wisdom and intelligence than the field of journalism education.

Conclusion

Taking stock of the great forces that converge to create an information society is the central purpose of the essays that make up this book. While there is no attempt here to forecast the future of the media society, there is an effort to consider where we are today and what influences have led us there. The trouble with futurists is not their fanciful visions of forthcoming developments, whether romantic or gloomy, but their unwillingness to consider seriously the many barriers to change.

Twenty years ago, Marshall McLuhan predicted the global village. He also rightly anticipated the convergence of print and broadcast media, but he did not pay much attention to impediments to change. Daniel Bell, in predicting an age of information, foresaw the massive growth of the communication sector and its ultimate challenge to manufacturing and agriculture. But neither McLuhan nor Bell anticipated the wrenching pace of change which has both short-term and long-run consequences. True, the media society is with us and more people are employed in communications activities than ever before, but it is also true that some media enterprises have withered and died; others have pruned their staff and resources in what is called "downsizing," while still others have thrived by providing new and needed services.

Thus the future of our information society will not be determined by sheer technological factors, but by human connections. It will inevitably be the nexus between people and media, the communication industry and its audiences—present and potential—that will govern the shape of things to come. Brilliant inventors and enthusiastic manufacturers notwithstanding, it is the needs and wants of the audience that will decide whether HDTV will survive and thrive, whether on-line databases will have a mass audience, and which media, old and new, will be with us in five or ten years.

There is a kind of ballet between the great forces of change: those that are technological and related to invention and those that are essentially economic, related to what people will pay for, as well as the regulatory rules of an organized society that act as pump-primer and traffic cop, depending on the issue or problem.

In writing the essays in this book, I have tried to be respectful of the several kinds of knowledge, some of it systematic, some of it impressionistic, that informs us about the media-people connection. Essentially research, which is the systematic assembly of information and knowledge, is about respect: respect for work that came before, respect for different ways of knowing that same terrain, and respect in listening to the hundreds of people who went into the equation that became this book.

I worry that many thoughtful people have abandoned this idea. In contributing new knowledge, too many of our contemporary commentators and scholars are either ignorant of what went before or openly contemptuous of it. Social scientists with their precise calibrations sneer at the broad brush strokes of historians. Critical theorists disdain what they think are the cowardly or wrong-headed conclusions of those with whom they disagree. The result in the academy, for those who look inside, is often a conceptual muddle, warring factions of media scholars and critics who have fundamental disagreements about all manner of ideas and issues.

When the stakes are as high as they are in the communication field, it is not unusual that there should be scholarly and critical disagreements, especially in a period of great social and technological change. But what is particularly disturbing is the fundamental lack of respect between and among people, which will not in the long run benefit anyone. By agreeing to disagree — to hold different views, even different "religious beliefs" about the nature, processes, and impact of media — we can still have a sensible "sorting out" of schools of thought, points of view, ways of knowing that can lead to a richer understanding. There need not be unified understanding, but we can agree that several "maps" of the field are useful to scholars, critics and, finally, the public.

Scholars and critics of the media, along with those insiders who own and operate media enterprises, owe it to the public, the consumers of media, to foster a continuing conversation that will help us all know and understand more about the troublesome and sometimes troubled institutions that make up our system of mass communication and freedom of expression.

References

Becker, Lee B., Jeffrey W. Fruit, and Susan L. Caudill. 1987. *Training and Hiring of Journalists.* Norwood, NJ: Ablex.

Gannett Center Journal, Vol. 2, No. 2, "The Making of Journalists." New York: Gannett Center for Media Studies, Spring 1988.

Johnstone, John W.C., Edward J. Slawski, and William W. Bowman. 1976. *News People: A Sociological Portrait of American Journalists and Their Work.* Urbana: University of Illinois Press.

Lichter, S. Robert, Stanley Rothman, Linda S. Lichter. 1986. *Media Elite.* Bethesda, MD: Adler & Adler.

Mills, Kay. 1988. *Place in the News: From the Women's Pages to the Front Page.* New York: Dodd, Mead.

Weaver, David H., Cleveland G. Wilhoit. 1986. *American Journalist: A Portrait of U.S. News People and Their Work.* Bloomington: Indiana University Press.

Index

About the Author

Everette E. Dennis is the Executive Director of the Gannett Center for Media Studies at Columbia University, the nation's first institute for the advanced study of mass communication and technological change. Before taking his current post, Dennis was Dean of the School of Journalism at the University of Oregon where he also headed the Project on the Future of Journalism Education, and served as national president of the Association for Education in Journalism and Mass Communication.

For nine years he was a member of the University of Minnesota School of Journalism and Mass Communication faculty, where he also served as director of the graduate studies program.

Author, coauthor, and editor of 14 books, Dennis has written and lectured widely about media and society issues, communication law, and other topics. His books include the popular text *Understanding Mass Communication*, coauthored with Melvin L. DeFleur, *Media, Freedom and Accountability, The Cost of Libel, The Media Society* and *Justice Black and the First Amendment*. He has also written more than 60 magazine and journal articles. His honors include three fellowships at Harvard University: the Liberal Arts Fellowship at Harvard Law School, a research fellowship at the J. F. Kennedy School of Government, and a special Nieman Foundation fellowship. In each instance he was the first journalism educator accorded these honors.

Dennis also has taught at Kansas State University and Northwestern University. He helped develop a unique program for behavioral science writers under federal grants in the 1960s and 1970s, and has worked both as a government information officer and a newspaper reporter.

He appears frequently on network television news and public affairs programs and is often quoted in major newspapers and magazines.

NOTES

NOTES

NOTES